John Townsend Trowbridge

Woodie Thorpe's Pilgrimage and other Stories

John Townsend Trowbridge

Woodie Thorpe's Pilgrimage and other Stories

ISBN/EAN: 9783337294212

Printed in Europe, USA, Canada, Australia, Japan

Cover: Foto ©Thomas Meinert / pixelio.de

More available books at **www.hansebooks.com**

WOODIE THORPE'S PILGRIMAGE

AND

OTHER STORIES

BY

J. T. TROWBRIDGE

AUTHOR OF "THE TIDE MILL STORIES" "SILVER MEDAL STORIES"
"START IN LIFE SERIES" ETC.

BOSTON
LEE AND SHEPARD PUBLISHERS
10 MILK STREET
1893

Woodie Thorpe's Pilgrimage

TO
ARTHUR TOWNSEND

CONTENTS

SISTER MARSH'S BEAU

UNCLE CALEB'S ROAN COLT

RODNEY HOBART'S MEMORY

NED LIFKIN'S FOREFINGER

FAY LIPPITT'S FOURTH OF JULY

THE BAMBERRY BOYS AND THEIR FLOCK OF SHEEP

ILLUSTRATIONS.

vii

WOODIE THORPE'S PILGRIMAGE

CHAPTER I

"YOU'VE MISSED YOUR MARK, YOUNGSTER!"

A ROUGH bundle of a boy, bounded by a narrow-brimmed felt hat that seemed too small for his head, a loose jacket too big for his body, and a pair of rubber boots too large for his feet, came tramping through the slush and melting snow of a desolate settlement in the wilds of Maine.

The day, though one of the shortest of the year, had been mild and bright; but the sun had sunk early behind the wooded hills, and with the sudden chill of the December dusk a gloom overspread the landscape, and a shadow fell on the boy's heart.

" I thought, from what he said, 'twas a good deal more of a place," he muttered to himself. " I don't see no such a great show for business here."

At the close of his toilsome all-day's journey on foot, a foreboding came over him that it was to end in some bitter disappointment. Since he had got so false an impression of the town, might he not have

been equally deceived in the person he was coming
to seek ?

" I can't believe that," he said.   " But what *did* he
mean by telling me he lived in a city ?   I'll ask that
man."   " If you please, sir, is this Salem ? "

" This is Salem, my boy."

The man, who was crossing the street, answered
the question in an off-hand, business-like way, and
continued his course.   The boy called after him
anxiously, —

" If you please, mister, do you know anybody living
here of the name of Turner ? "

" Oh, yes ; everybody knows Turner."   The man
stopped and pointed.   " That yellow house yonder,
just before you get to the bridge."

" Thank you," said the boy gratefully ; and he
walked on with a lighter heart and quicker step.   If
he could find his friend he felt sure that all would
be well, and the mistake he had made in thinking Salem so much more of a place would be explained.

He went around, in a humble manner, to the side
door of the yellow house, and knocked hardly louder
than his heart was knocking with hope and fear in
his breast.   Yes, Mr. Turner lived there, and he was
in, he was told by a woman who opened the door ;
and then an old man with a bushy gray beard came
forward.

Again the boy's spirit felt a chill of misgiving :
the place and people didn't seem at all such as he

had imagined the home and family of his good friend to be.

"Did you want anything of me?" said the old man with the bushy gray beard.

"I want to see Mr. Turner," faltered the boy.

"I am Mr. Turner."

In his little close-rimmed felt hat, buttoned jacket, and big rubber boots, the boy stood there in the December dusk, and looked up with a jaded, anxious, distressed face at the old man looking down.

"It's another Mr. Turner I want," said he. "Maybe he's your son."

"I have no son," said the old man; "and there is no other Mr. Turner, that I know of, in this town."

The boy looked dazed for a moment; then said, in a forced voice, "They told me this was Salem."

"And so it is," said the man.

"Well, *he* lives in Salem — the Mr. Turner I've come all the way from Bushfork to see. I've his card." And, fumbling under his jacket, the boy produced a worn and creased bit of pasteboard, bearing a partly obliterated name and address.

"Here it is. I've carried it in my pocket so long I don't know as you can read it. But that's the name," said the boy, as if throwing the responsibility for all blunders upon the tattered card — "Nathan P. Turner, Salem; and that's the man I want to find."

"There's no such man here, nor in this part of the country, I'm very sure." And the wrong Mr. Turner

took what was left of the right Mr. Turner's card between his thumb and finger.   " Mamie, hand me my
spectacles, or else read this name yourself.   What
do you make out ? " as a small girl came forward and
scrutinized it sharply by the waning light.

" *Nathan P. Turner, Salem,*" she read, without
much difficulty.

" Yes, that's it ! " cried the boy eagerly.   " He
must be here somewhere."

But the old man shook his head.

" Is that all, Mamie ?   Git me my glasses."

" *Salem, Ms.,*" said the girl.

"*Ms. ?*   What's *Ms. ?* " the old man demanded.

" I don't know what *Ms.* stands for," replied the
boy.   " But I kind o' thought it might mean the part
of the town where he lives."

" I'll tell you what it means ! " exclaimed the old
man, having adjusted his spectacles.   " *Salem, Ms.,*
is *Salem, Massachusetts,* boy !   This is Salem in the
State of Maine.   You've missed your mark, youngster, by nigh onto a couple o' hundred mile."

CHAPTER II

THE WRONG SALEM

FORTUNATELY the boy was well propped in his extensive rubber boots; otherwise he might have tumbled over, so sudden and stunning was this blow.

"Salem, Massachusetts," the old man repeated, "that's the place ye want. Hain't ye got no more gumption than to come hunting for it in the wilderness of Maine?"

"I thought *Mass.* stood for Massachusetts," said the boy, in a faint voice. "I never heard of anybody putting *Ms.* for it before."

"Neither did I, gran'pa," spoke up the girl, inclined to take his part. "Of course it's *Mass.*"

"It's gener'ly *Mass.*, but sometimes *Ms.*," replied the old man, giving back the card. "*Me.* stands for Maine. If it was *Salem, Me.*, now, your man would be here, and you would be all right. It seems a little matter at the tail-end of a name; but that difference of a single letter looms up in your case, young chap — le' me see. A good ninety mile to Portland, and over a hundred from there to Boston. Salem — your Salem — is this side of Boston. But it's a round hundred and eighty mile from here, if 'tis a rod. That's what that one little letter signifies for *you*."

The boy was so pitiful a picture, disheartened, uncertain, trembling, with the winter night closing in upon him, that the old man, after regarding him a moment, continued, in a kinder tone, —

"You don't know much of the world, do ye, not to have found out there's more'n one Salem in it."

"I don't know nothing of the world," the boy answered, out of the very depths of humility. "I never was away from home before."

"Where is your home?"

"'Tain't nowhere now. '*Twas* over in Bushfork."

"Well, why ain't it there now?"

"My cousin, Tom Barrus, that I lived with, he died last summer; and now his wife has married another man that don't like me, and there ain't no more room in the house for me." And a sob broke into the boy's voice, as at the memory of wrongs.

"So you've run away!"

"No, sir; I haven't run away. They've no claim on me; and when they treated me so I couldn't stand it any longer, then I left. It was this morning. I've been travelling, and I've come to the wrong Salem, after all!"

The boy was whimpering miserably on the door-steps. The drip from the roof was already freezing about his feet. Behind him rose the forest-covered spurs of Mt. Abraham, growing darker and darker against the cold, clear sky; and a dreary wind was rising, giving some promise of a storm.

" What's your name ? " the old man inquired.

" Woodie Thorpe. My whole first name is Woodman; but folks sometimes call me Woodie Barrus, since I've lived so long with my Cousin Tom."

" Haven't you any parents or other relatives ? "

" My father was killed by a falling tree, four years ago; and my mother died the next spring. I suppose I may have other relatives besides Cousin Tom somewhere, but I don't know where."

"Do ask him into the house, and don't keep the poor boy standing there, with the door open ! " exclaimed the woman within, in a tone of mingled kindness and impatience, for the chilly wind was penetrating the house.

So Woodie Thorpe was taken into a warm little kitchen, where a supper of bear-meat was frying, the odor of which was incense to his hungry soul.

" But who is this other Mr. Turner you're in search of ? " the old man asked, as he gave him a seat by the stove.

" He's a man who comes to Bushfork for hunting and fishing sometimes. He came last summer, expecting Tom would go into the woods with him. Tom was a regular guide; but Tom was sick, and so I went."

" You ! " and the old man looked down with incredulous surprise at the small stranger. " How old be ye ? Not above twelve or thirteen, to judge by your looks."

"I hain't kep' track o' my age very well," Woodie
replied.   "But Cousin Tom said he calculated I was
fourteen last March."

"And could you act as a guide? A mite like
you?" said the old man.

"Well, I did!"

The boy's face lighted up as he told his story
there by the comfortable fire, with Mamie and her
grandfather to sympathize with him, and the woman
pausing in her work to listen.

"He took sick in the woods, and we was seven mile
from any settlement, and I took care of him and
brought him out, — and he was the best friend I ever
had!" Woodie exclaimed, with a throb of emotion.
"And when he left, he gi' me that card, and told me if
I ever wanted help of any kind, to let him know.   He
would have taken me home with him, but Tom
wasn't willing; and we didn't expect then Tom was
going to die.   I wished afterwards I *had* gone; and
when I found I couldn't stay there much longer, I
looked at the card ever so many times a day, and
asked which way Salem was; and when I heard a
man might walk to it between sun and sun, I just
made up my mind and started.   But the walking
was awful, and I missed my way two or three times;
and now," he added, with another break in his voice,
"it seems I've missed it altogether, and might about
as well have gone to the North Pole!"

"Oh, no! not quite so bad as that," said the old
man.   "You're in a better haven than you'd be apt

to find up there, this time of year. We can keep ye over night, — can't we, Marthy? — and give ye supper and breakfast, and maybe some good advice in the morning."

"Yes, we can do that," said the woman, placing the supper on the table ; while the young girl looked at Woodie Thorpe with eyes that shone with sympathy.

The advice the old man had to bestow upon the young traveller the next morning was, that he should go back to his home in Bushfork, and make the best of it. But Woodie hung his head.

"I can't go back there," he said. "They would treat me worse than ever now. Which is the way to that other Salem — away off in Massachusetts?"

"You don't think of going there, do you?" exclaimed the old man.

"I don't know what I shall do. But I may as well move along. What's the name of the next place on the road?"

"The first place of any importance is Farmington. That's twenty mile from here. But you can strike the railroad nigher than that."

"I don't know what I want of the railroad, with two good legs of my own," said Woodie, ashamed to admit that he couldn't afford to ride. Then, putting his hand in his pocket, he asked how much he owed for his entertainment.

"We sometimes take pay from travellers," the old man answered, scratching his gray head. "But I guess you ain't much overburdened with cash."

"I don't happen to have more'n I can carry," said the boy, with a smile. "But I ain't a beggar." And he took out some small change.

"Put up yer chink! put up yer chink!" cried the old man. "We couldn't take nothing from a boy like you, no way in the world. You'll want what you've got to take ye to Farmington and keep ye over night. I don't calc'late you'll go much further. Maybe ye can find something to do there. Wish we had something for ye here. Never mind yer thanks, sonny. You're quite welcome, quite welcome, to what little we've done for ye."

CHAPTER III

A TERRIBLE JOURNEY

WITH a full heart and over-full eyes, Woodie Thorpe left these kind people, and took the Farmington road, with the other Mr. Turner's dilapidated card in his pocket, and eighty-nine cents in money to keep it company.

He had left Bushfork, the day before, with ninety-seven cents, and had paid eight cents for the crackers and cheese he ate on his journey. With what remained he now set off, in the depth of winter, with only the rudest tracks before him, over the frozen slush and half-trodden snow, to walk to that other Salem, a hundred and eighty miles away.

This was his secretly formed resolution, which, however, he did not fully admit even to himself. The longing for his friend, whom it would be such joy and good fortune to find, was like a powerful magnet in his breast, drawing him on ; and while his strength lasted, neither forest solitudes, nor dreary stretches of unfrequented roads, nor blinding snow-storms, nor hunger and weariness and cold — and he had to encounter all these — could turn him' from his purpose.

Only twice on that terrible journey did he sleep inside a human habitation, but barns and sheds and stacks afforded him his only shelter from the night and wintry wind.

He had no overcoat ; and water had begun to find its way into his big rubber boots, even on that first day of thaw. Fortunately, there were not many such days ; but it was not long before the snow itself followed the insidious water, and kept his feet wet and cold.

He had set out with a manly determination not to beg, but his little store of money was soon gone ; and then, when he asked for a job of sawing wood to pay for his breakfast or supper, and found himself often repulsed, as if he had been a common tramp, the real shame and hardship of his journey began.

Occasionally he got a ride on a pung or wood-sled going his way, and that he considered an immense help. And he found a few kind people, who listened to his story, gave him food and shelter, and allowed him to warm his feet by their fires ; but the farther he went, the more miserable and shabby he appeared, and the more he was treated like a vagabond and impostor, undeserving of sympathy.

He was three days in reaching Portland; then three days more in reaching Newburyport, by which time he had become so footsore and worn and jaded, and so unenterprising in getting rides, that it was not until the afternoon of the eighth day from the wrong Salem that he crossed the bridge from Beverly, and entered the streets of the right Salem at last.

It chanced that it was Christmas Day, but as dismal a Christmas as one often sees. A thin fog was driving in from the sea, and a drizzling rain was falling. Rain and fog froze upon every object they touched, and trees and fences and house-fronts were sheathed in ice. The walks were slippery, except where one's foot broke through the newly formed crust at the crossings, into slush and water and mud below.

Such was the afternoon when, at three o'clock, the little traveller, after much inquiry and going astray, turned into the yard of a fine old house on Chestnut Street. It must have been beautiful there in summer, and the place suited well his notion of what *his* Mr. Turner's home should be ; but it looked dreary enough in the mist and drizzle, and the bare elms under which he passed whistled in the wind, and creaked in their icy mail.

There was not much strength left in the boy's tired limbs, nor hope in his heart ; but with what little he had he mounted the broad stone steps, and gave the bell a spasmodic pull. As he did so, you might have seen that he staggered a little, and kept his hold of the bell-handle, as if to save himself from reeling backwards off the steps. He had had nothing but a crust to eat since morning ; and for two days he had been as near starvation as a boy could well be, and keep on his feet.

The door was opened; and out of the warm hall with a whiff of soft, summer-like air, stepped a boy of about Woodie Thorpe's own age, but belonging, you would almost have said, to another species. He was plump and dry and sleek; his hair was carefully parted on one side, over a full, fair forehead; his dainty necktie was in a perfect knot, and his polished shoes shone.

An amazing contrast was Woodie. His cheeks were sunken, his eyes had a glassy glitter, his hair was unkempt, his face unwashed; his hands were a grimmy pair of paws. He was drenched to the skin, and his shapeless hat and ragged jacket were already stiffening with frost. His soiled trousers disappeared in the tops of his dilapidated boots, which made a flapping sound without, and gave forth a churning sound from within, as the soaked feet took a step toward the other boy.

"Does Mr. Turner — Mr. Nathan P. Turner — live here?" Poor Woodie put his question in a faint and anxious breath, as if his life depended on the answer.

"He does," said the fair and sleek boy coldly, with a frown at the little wretch who had ventured to ring the street-door bell.

"Can I see him?"

As Woodie faltered forth this second question, the mighty difference between this boy's prosperity and his own misery, and the stupendous folly he had been guilty of in making such a journey to find a man who had probably forgotten him, and would no doubt frown, even as this boy frowned, at sight of his wretchedness, — all this came over him in a way that prepared his sinking heart for the prompt and cold response.

" I don't see how you can, for he isn't at home."

" When will he be home ? " Woodie asked.

" Can't say.   He's gone to Boston."

Woodie fumbled with numb fingers for the limp remnant of his precious card, and was gasping for breath enough to say, " He told me to find him ; may I come in and wait ? " when the sleek boy remarked : —

"You shouldn't ring at the front door of gentlemen's houses.   Go to the back door if you want anything."

And the front door was abruptly closed, shutting one boy within, with the warmth and Christmas cheer, and the other without, in the wintry wind and freezing rain.

CHAPTER IV

SHUT OUT

Woodie Thorpe did not go to the back door, as he was bidden — why should he, since his friend was not at home ? — but wandered away again, watched from a window by the boy within, until he disappeared in the fog and drizzle down the street.

Now this young gentleman was Clifford Turner, a younger brother of Nathan P., and by no means the hard-hearted child of fortune his conduct may have made him appear. The country was at that time infested by tramps, who wore out the patience of the most benevolent householders ; and this was not the first time poor Woodie had been taken for one of that worthless crew.

Besides, Clifford Turner was expecting a friend of his to come to their Christmas dinner ; and hearing the door-bell, he had gone himself to admit him, when he found our drenched and tattered young traveller instead.

But his friend came in a short time ; it was Milton Morris, from the boarding-school. Other friends and relatives were already gathered in the commodious old house, and just at dark, — it grew dark very early that night, — Nathan P. arrived from Boston.

Clifford knew very well when he was expected, and had been needlessly sparing of information in response to poor Woodie's inquiries. He had learned that the most annoying of all tramps was he who ascertained in advance the names of people living in houses he proposed to visit, and it never occurred to him that our little adventurer from Bushfork could have any honest business with his brother.

Woodie wandered away hopeless and forlorn, and ready to sink down at any moment with weariness and want of food. He saw the interiors of happy homes lighted up, one by one, as the early winter night set in, and caught glimpses of bright children in the glow of lamps and open fires before the curtains were drawn, as if to shut him out even from the sight of such warmth and bliss.

He was faint and giddy, with a dull ache in his head and despair in his heart, and senses fast becoming dulled by the severity of the sleety storm. With no other object in view but to pass away the time until his friend should return home, he walked about by the waning daylight, and then by the glimmering gaslight, as the street lamps were lighted, and at length sought a dismal shelter under some coal-sheds by a wharf.

By this time the Christmas festivities were at their height in the old Turner mansion. A goodly company of old and young surrounded the table, at one end of which Nathan P. himself cracked his pleasant jokes and carved the goose. He was a

short, rosy, jovial bachelor, evidently the pride of
his widowed mother, and a favorite with his brothers
and sisters and cousins, who were present on the
cheerful occasion.

"I was never better in my life," he said, in reply
to some one who spoke of his glowing health,
"though I am not quite so well as I expect to be
when I get a little farther along with the dinner.
I haven't been troubled by a visit from my old
enemy since I was in the Maine woods last summer."

"We heard you had a rheumatic attack up there,"
said Cousin Belle, from Springfield. "How did it
happen?"

"It was all owing to the absurd circumstance that
I couldn't call a hack in the middle of a swamp,
when a rainstorm came on. It's a ridiculous over-
sight that hacks are not provided in such cases, and
I had to suffer for it."

"Tell how you happened to go into the woods
with only a boy for a guide," said Clifford. "Milton would like to hear about that."

"It was because the guide I depended on chanced
to be sick," said Nathan P.; "but I had gone up
there for a little taste of wild life, and I meant to
have it, even if I went into the woods alone. I had
been there before, and didn't need a guide as much
as I needed some one to wait on me and cook for
me, paddle me about the lake, and help me fight
mosquitoes. Tom sent his boy to find me another

man ; and when he came back without one, he — the
boy — looked at me so wistfully, remarking that *he*
knew how to cook trout and venison, and make
coffee, — and he was altogether such a bright, active,
helpful little fellow, though hardly fourteen years
old, and small for his age, — that I made up my
mind at once.

"'Tom,' I said, 'if you can't go yourself, I'll have
no guide but your boy here.'

"'He'll do you good service,' says Tom, 'though
I didn't like to say so till you had seen whether you
could do better.'

"Then you should have seen that youngster's
face light up! He was fond of adventures of that
sort, and I learned afterwards that he wasn't very
happy at home. The family were only relatives of
his ; and though Tom was kind, Tom's wife was a
shrew, and made life squally for him sometimes.
Besides, he seemed to have taken a liking to me the
year before ; I was there then, and made him some
little presents, which I had forgotten all about, but
which, it appeared, he remembered, as if he had
never tasted caramels nor handled a four-bladed
pocket-knife before.

"I passed the night in their log cabin there at
Bushfork, and early the next morning, with Little
Barrus — that's what I called him ; his adopted
father was Tom Barrus — and another still smaller
boy of Tom's, to help us with our *toter*, I put out
for the old camping-ground. You know what a *toter*

is?" Nathan P. went on, looking over at Clifford's friend Milton. "It's a sort of narrow sled, or drag, by which you carry your luggage and provisions and ammunition along the trail through the woods, where nothing on wheels can go — let alone hacks. We had a horse to haul it; and the littlest Barrus rode the horse, while I and my juvenile guide tramped behind, or at the side of the *toter*, when there was danger of its being upset by the roots and stumps amongst which we took our somewhat winding way. The boy and the horse were to take us to our camp, leave us there, and return for us at the end of ten days.

"It looked like rain when we started, but little did I expect *such* a rain! We had gone about four miles, and were in the middle of a great swamp, when it began to pour. We might have gone back; but as it was only three miles farther to the lake, where there was a good hut to shelter us, we kept on, and reached there about noon, as wet as if we had just come out of the lake itself, like so many muskrats.

"Rubber coat? I had one, but it was in my trunk, and my trunk was on the *toter*, and I was pretty well drenched before I could have got at it, so sudden was the shower. Then, thinking it would hold up before long, and I might get dry walking, I didn't take out my blanket at all. But there was no hold up to that rain; it poured, as Little Barrus said, as if the plug was out, all that day and all that night.

"The hut was damp; and somebody had been there and burned up all the dry wood Barrus had provided, and we had a great deal of trouble in making a very poor fire. The result was that when I awoke the next morning, I could scarcely move hand or foot; I was one entire rheumatic ache and cramp!

"Well, there I was, disabled, and no more capable of walking back to Tom's than I was of flying back. The horse and boy had returned the afternoon before. Little Barrus would have gone for me if I had let him, but it was a hard road to travel, and it would have taken him all day to go and return; and there was no doctor there, not even an apothecary's shop, nor any nurse to be had. I had some medicines with me, and I had to be my own doctor. The hut was my hospital, and Little Barrus my nurse.

"And a capital nurse he was!" Nathan P. went on, carving for himself at last. "Such constant, kind attention I never saw in anybody else, except my own mother," with a glance at the fine old lady at the other end of the table, who listened to his story now for the twentieth time, perhaps, with glistening eyes. "He was more anxious about me than I was about myself, and he seemed to know by intuition what was wanted of him. He had everything to do; to cook his own meals, and mine too when I was able to eat, get wood and water, and run to wait on me whenever I called; and he never failed me once.

He was so faithful, so sympathetic, that the mere sight of him or the sound of his voice was a comfort. I do believe," added Nathan P., with a tremor in his lowered tones, "if it had been necessary for him to give his own life to save mine, he would have done it cheerfully.

"Well, fine weather, after two days of rain, good nursing, and good doctoring, — I must take a little credit to myself, — brought me through; and I didn't stay very long to fish, I assure you, after I was once more on my feet. We caught a few trout and shot a few partridges; and then, the horse coming for us, we beat a retreat.

"I never so regretted parting with a boy in my, life " —

Nathan P. was going on with his story, when a servant came in to say that some one was asking for him at the kitchen door.

"For me ? I have but just begun my dinner ! Who is it ? What does he want ? "

"He looks like a tramp, and a pretty miserable kind of one," replied the woman.

"That reminds me," said Clifford; "one came to the front door for you an hour or two ago. The hardest-looking case I've seen for a great while! not much bigger than I am, though he looked almost as old as the Old Man of the Sea."

"Two, eh ? and it isn't a very good day for tramps, either ! " said Nathan P., laying down his knife and fork.

"Perhaps it's the same one," explained the woman. "This one is little, and it may be hard times that makes him look so old."

"Nathan has but just begun to eat his dinner," observed the old lady. "If it is anybody who really has business with him, he can wait or call again in an hour. But if he has only come begging, give him something to eat and send him away."

At that Nathan P. settled down once more to his knife and fork.

"Don't let the interruption spoil your story," said Cousin Belle. "I am interested in that boy."

"There isn't much more to tell," Nathan P. resumed. "That boy actually shed tears when I left him at Bushfork; and I am not ashamed to confess that I had a slight mistiness of vision. I proposed to bring him home with me, but Tom couldn't agree to it; more than that, Tom's wife — who had always said he was a burden to the family, and not worth the salt in his porridge — came to a very sudden conclusion that he was worth keeping. Still I think I could have got him off, but for Barrus's sickness. He was much worse when we came out of the woods, and Little Barrus thought he ought to stay and help the family."

Here the servant woman re-entered. "He says his name is Thorpe, and that you met him out here,— in the rain, I think he said,— and told him to come and find you." Such was her imperfect understanding of poor Woodie's story.

" Thorpe ? I don't know any Thorpe ! " said Nathan P. "And I haven't met anybody in the rain, nor told anybody to come and find me. He is either an impostor, or he has come to the wrong house by mistake."

" I will tell him you don't know any Thorpe, and that he must have come to the wrong house," said the woman, once more retiring.

"What would you have done with him if you had brought him home ? " Clifford wished to know.

" I had hardly thought as far as that," replied Nathan P. " I could have given him work in the shoe-factory at all events, and perhaps have done better than that. I would have sent him to school, if he had shown an inclination that way, for precious little schooling did he ever get in those backwoods of Maine. Then I might have taken him into the bank. But " —

" O Mr. Turner ! " exclaimed the woman, suddenly reappearing, with a frightened face, " I wish you would step here ! "

" What has happened ? " cried Nathan P., rising abruptly from his Christmas dinner.

" That boy — for he is nothing but a boy — when I told him you didn't know him, and he had come to the wrong house," the woman went on excitedly, " he just turned away, with the most pitiful face I ever saw, without a word, — he had already refused the food I offered him, — turned and started for the street, but slipped, and fell right there by the steps.

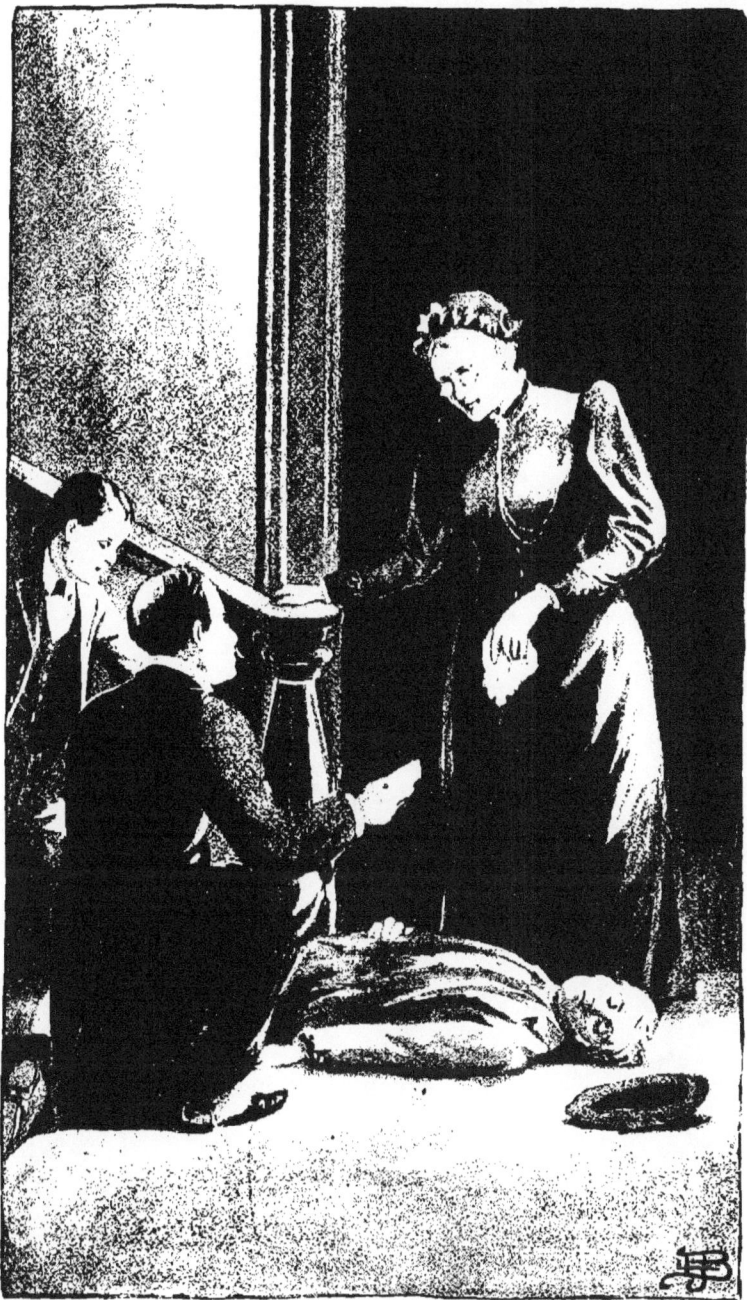

"It's little Barrus."—Page 25.

I waited for him to get up; but he did not stir, and I believe he's in a dead swoon."

"Thorpe? Thorpe?" Nathan P. repeated, hurriedly following her. "It is very strange!"

"There was another name he gave," the woman added, as they passed through the kitchen, — "Woodman, or Woodford. I couldn't understand all he said."

The cook was already lifting the boy over the threshold. His clothes were frozen stiff, his head and limbs drooped heavily; there was nothing in the wan, worn face that Nathan P. recognized. One of his lifeless hands unclasped, and a bit of crumpled paper fell on the floor. Clifford, who had run to the spot out of curiosity, picked it up.

"What is it?" his brother demanded, and snatched it from his hand as he was puzzling over it. "My card!" he exclaimed, in amazement.

At the same time the stiff, frozen, shapeless hat fell off, and exposed the boy's pallid forehead and straggling hair.

"Woodman! did he say Woodman?" Nathan P. repeated, stooping over him, and trying to remember. "Woodie!" he cried, in sudden surprise and consternation. That name came back to him, though he could not remember Thorpe. "Mother! Jane! it's my boy-nurse! it's Little Barrus!"

CHAPTER V

THE RIGHT MR. TURNER

It was a strange interruption to a Christmas dinner! For a while the table was deserted, and everybody crowded to get a glimpse of the hero of the story in which all had been so much interested a few minutes before.

"I never dreamed he could be the one!" said Clifford, in bitter self-reproach. "He must have been reaching for that card when I shut the door in his face."

Woodie Thorpe did not yet know what had happened to him. But warmth and restoratives soon brought him back to a consciousness of pain, and of a great joy.

Bending over him, and rubbing his benumbed limbs, where he lay between dry blankets, with a jug of hot water at his feet, — bending over him, with a face of love and pity, and lips uttering words of affection and cheer, was the one friend he had in the world, — the friend he had made his long and terrible journey, in the depths of winter, from the wilds of Maine, to find, — the friend who, he now knew, could never have meant to deny him, and drive him from his door.

"You are all right now, aren't you, Little Barrus? You know me, don't you?" Nathan P. was saying.

"You are Mr. Turner!" said Woodie gratefully. "I thought I never should get to see you!"

Then, after a while, as Nathan P. continued to rub life into his limbs with warm hands, and breathe hope into his heart with kind words, he added, in broken sentences, "I had about given you up. And I don't know how I found you — or did you find me? It seems as if I had been asleep!"

Nathan P. did not tell him how near he had been to sleeping the sleep from which there is no awaking in this world.

Clifford now came forward, eager, sympathetic, bringing a bowl of soup, followed by his mother, announcing that a warm bath was ready.

"A little nourishment before the bath, don't you say so, Little Barrus?" asked Nathan P., with a smile.

"Splendid soup, as hot as you can take it!" cried Clifford, offering to feed the patient with a spoon. "You won't object to that."

Woodie did not object in the least. "Oh, how good!" he murmured thankfully, as he sipped it. "Oh, how it warms me up!" And with the blankets about him he sat up in bed, supported in the arms of his friend.

Clifford's white hand trembled with joyful eagerness as he fed the hungry boy.

"Why didn't you tell me who you were, when I

saw you at the door?" he asked, still with stings of
remorse. "I hadn't the faintest idea!"

"I tried — I was going to — but somehow I didn't
have time," said Woodie, between spoonfuls.

"Where did you go after that?" Nathan P. inquired.

"I just wandered about, and got under some
black sheds," said Woodie. "I didn't feel cold any
more. I felt numb and sleepy. That frightened
me, for I had heard of people feeling that way when
they were freezing. So I got up, and came back
here — or did I dream it? I can hardly think how
it happened; I am confused yet!"

"You didn't dream it," replied Nathan P. "But
somebody else was near making a fearful mistake!
I had forgotten your name was Thorpe: I always
called you by the name of the man you lived with,
you remember. Tom Barrus. How is Tom?"

"He's dead," Woodie answered, with a faint
smack after Clifford's last spoonful.

Thinking that, if a little soup was good for him,
a great deal would be better, Clifford would have
liked to feed him about a gallon; and he brought a
second bowlful, proud and delighted to do so much,
and disappointed because Nathan P. would not let
him spoon it out.

"He has had enough for the present," said the
elder brother, tucking the warm blankets about
Woodie, to foster the glow that was beginning to
suffuse his limbs. "We mustn't kill him with kindness. Did you say Tom was dead?"

"He died a week or two after you left," said Woodie. "And she married Reub Hawley. After that I got kind o' crowded out; and I thought of you, and heard that Salem wasn't very far from Bushfork, and started to walk to it, with just a little of the money left that you gave me, — she had taken the rest. But I went to the wrong Salem ; there's no city there, only a town, with a few houses scattered over a rough country."

"You went to Salem in Maine ! " exclaimed Nathan P.

"Yes, and then I started to walk to this Salem," said Woodie. "And I walked all the way, only once in a while I got a lift, the first few days. And I got out of money — and " —

Tears came into his eyes at the recollection of his sufferings on that dreadful journey.

"You poor Little Barrus ! " said Nathan P., with tears of pity in his own eyes. "You have had a terrible time ! But now you have found the right Salem, and you shall never be out of money again, as long as I have any."

"I felt sure you would be my friend ! " And Woodie began to cry very softly with his newly found happiness.

"You took care of me in the Maine woods," Nathan P. went on, "and now I am going to take care of you. I wonder if I shall make half as good a nurse ! "

"You were a very good doctor, I remember," said

Woodie, with a faint smile, which grew fainter and fainter as he dropped off wearily into a deep sleep.

He had found the right Salem, indeed, and not one friend only, but many, one of the most generous and devoted being that same Clifford, who had shut the street door in his face at first. Thanks to the good nursing he received, he was on his feet the next day, a little weak and sore from the sufferings he had undergone in his weary pilgrimage, but otherwise comfortable, and certainly very grateful and very glad.

He did not go back to Bushfork until long after, when he revisited the old place in company with Mr. Nathan P. Turner, who was then president of the bank in which he was himself a rising clerk.

AUNT ABBY'S DIAMOND RING.

CHAPTER I

MARTIN GOWER'S ERRAND

A FEW years ago, there lived in a small house on Myrtle Street a widow named Abigail Tolley. She had thin gray hair, the pale, nervous face of an invalid, and she hobbled about the house with a cane. She was fretful at times, yet she had one of the kindest hearts in the world.

There lived with her at that time an orphan niece, Susie, a girl about sixteen years old, and a boy named Martin Gower, — a nephew on her husband's side, — whom she had taken into her house after he had been turned out of doors by a drunken step-father.

Martin was seventeen; a bright, resolute, good hearted fellow, though not without the faults common to boys of his age.

I am afraid he was not grateful enough for all the widow's kindness. He knew that she could not afford to support him in idleness ; and yet he sometimcs

performed very unwillingly the small household tasks
required of him. He was always absorbed in some
plan of his own ; and he did not like being reminded,
in a fretful voice, that he had neglected to cut the
morrow's kindling-wood, or to fill the lodgers' water-
pitchers.

Martin had lived with the widow about a year,
when he came home from school one afternoon and
found her unusually low-spirited and nervous.

"What's the matter with Aunt Abby?" he said
in a whisper to Susie, as he passed her in the entry.

" One of her *poor* fits," replied Susie.   " She thinks
we're all going to the alms-house."

" Well, let's go then, and have done with it !" said
Martin. " What's the use of so much fuss about
it ? "

But though Susie could speak unkindly of her
aunt, she did not like that Martin should. "You
forget all she has done for you !" she exclaimed
reproachfully.

" Not much danger of that, when she and you
remind me of it so often !" he retorted.

" You didn't take the ashes from Mr. Hobart's
stove this morning," Susie called after him, as he
was passing in.

"Of course, there's something I didn't do !" said
Martin carelessly.

" And I had to do it for you !" she added.

" And I guess it didn't hurt you !" was his last
word.

He was mounting the stairs, when Mrs. Tolley's feeble, querulous voice was heard in her little sitting-room.

"Susie! Martin! Come here, both of you!"

"I can't come now; see what she wants," Martin said to Susie.

"You must come!" cried Susie, having spoken to her aunt.

And Martin, with a scowl on his brow, entered the widow's room.

She sat in her easy-chair by the window, with an open letter in her lap.

"Children," she said, with quivering lips, and in a trembling voice, "here is something I didn't mean to speak to you about; but I find I must. This letter, Susie, came to-day when you were out. It is from your brother Luther."

"Is it bad news?" Susie inquired anxiously.

"It's the same old story. He is having no end of trouble with his patent. I have sent him money, and sent him money, thinking every time it was the last. Now he must have thirty dollars at once. But I haven't thirty dollars in the world, and I don't know where to borrow it. That patent of his will ruin us all, and I wish it was at the bottom of the sea!"

Susie cried. Martin reached out his hand for the letter.

"May I read it?" he asked.

"Dear, yes! if you can have the heart to."

But if the boy had the heart, he did not have the

skill, and the letter was finally turned over to Susie, who dried her eyes and read it aloud.

It was a simple and affecting story of struggle, hardship, and disappointed hopes. But now the young inventor believed himself on the very threshold of success. He had put off appealing again to his aunt, until driven by actual necessity to take the step which he feared would be as troublesome to her as it was distressing to him. Could she once more send him a little money, and still put faith in his gratitude and fidelity?

"Now you see how it is," said the widow, when Susie had finished the letter. "I have four or five just such letters as that; only the last ones show more and more how the poor boy has suffered. I have sent him every dollar I could spare; and now we cannot, without great sacrifices, send him more. What can be done?"

"Oh, I don't know, Aunt Abby!" said Susie. "I am sure Luther has meant to do right. You never told us you were sending him money."

"No, for I didn't want to trouble you. You were going to say something, Martin?"

The boy was struggling with some strong emotion. All his generous impulses were roused.

"You have done everything you could, I know!" he replied. "And I never even guessed what was troubling you so! Isn't there something *I* can do?"

"For what?" said Aunt Abby.

"To help you and Luther — to do my share!" he exclaimed.

"My boy!" said the widow, in a faltering voice, "you help me — you and Susie both help me — when you show your sympathy and good-will."

Martin remembered with shame how grudgingly he had often done the few small duties assigned to him in the home of his benefactress. She continued, —

"Next to mortgaging the house, which I can't bear the thought of, there is one last resort."

She took from her pocket a small velvet-covered jewel-case, and lifting the cover, showed a ring.

"This was my daughter's. It was her wedding-ring. I have kept it sacredly since she died. But now I suppose I must part with it. I hoped it would be yours some day, Susie."

"Oh, don't mind about me!"

But the girl's eyes sparkled at sight of the jewel.

"Is the stone a diamond?" Martin inquired.

"Yes, and a fine one, though not very large. It ought to bring sixty dollars. Now, Martin, I am going to confide it to your care. I would go myself to dispose of it, if I could afford the expense of a carriage. But you may see what you can do first. Avoid the pawnbrokers; go to any respectable jewellers. You may sell it for fifty dollars, if you can't get more; but I'd rather borrow thirty or forty dollars on it, than sell it at any price."

The boy looked anxious and excited as Aunt Abby

put the case into his hands, with instructions how to act.

"I wish Susie could go with me!" he said, with a sense of the responsibility laid upon him.

"She might, but she has so much to do here at home. Now, Martin, I rely upon your fidelity and judgment. Get the money if you can; if not, bring back the ring. Be sure not to lose either that or the money."

"I won't lose anything!" said Martin confidently.

She also gave him a card, on which she had written, —

"The bearer of this, Martin Gower, aged seventeen, is authorized to dispose of a diamond ring for me."

To this her name and address were signed, so that he might not be suspected of having stolen the jewel.

Then, after he was gone, Susie and her aunt talked over the affair and waited for his return.

"You couldn't trust many boys that way!" said Susie, having set the table for their frugal supper.

"What do you mean?" asked Aunt Abby, who sat watching from the window.

"Oh, just think what a temptation it would be to a dishonest boy!" said Susie. "Forty or fifty dollars! That's a big sum for a wild young fellow to have burning in his pocket."

"But Martin is not a wild young fellow," Mrs. Tolley replied.

"No, lucky for us! You would never see your

ring again, or your money, if he was. I wonder how it will seem to him to have fifty dollars in his hands all at once."

Now, Susie, talking in this way, did not mean to make her aunt nervous. But it was time for them to be expecting Martin's return; and as the widow sat watching, and saw the street grow dark, and no Martin appeared, it took but a hint to agitate her.

"Martin is honest; I am sure he is honest," she said, in a trembling voice. "But he may have met with some accident. Or — I don't know — a large sum of money would be a temptation to almost any boy, I suppose."

"I would trust Martin with hundreds!" Susie exclaimed. "He isn't perfect, by any means; the trouble with him is *he don't think;* but at heart, Aunt Abby, Martin Gower is as true as any boy in this world!"

She spoke warmly; for, notwithstanding their little disputes, she was Martin's steadfast friend.

Her earnest words allayed for a while the fears she had raised in her aunt's mind. But now the lighting of the street-lamps gave the watching widow an uneasy sense of the coming on of night.

"Surely," she said, "he ought to be here by this time! I wish you had gone with him, Susie. Perhaps he was *afraid* of being tempted, when he asked to have your company. Oh, what shall I do if he doesn't come back?"

" He'll come back safe enough ! It's a poor compliment you pay him," Susie added, " when you suspect him so, because he is a little late."

" I don't mean to wrong him," the widow said,
after opening the window, in order to take a long
look down the street. " But he may have fallen in
with some of his old companions. You know he had
some dangerous acquaintances before I took him ;
and it has been hard for him to keep clear of
them."

The table had been kept waiting an hour ; and
Susie herself, it must be confessed, was beginning to
be anxious about Martin.

Still another hour passed. Susie and her aunt had
gone through with the formality of sitting at the
table ; but they had scarcely tasted anything on
it ; they could not eat while they were waiting for
Martin.

" I will go out and look for him," said Susie, at nine
o'clock.

" That won't do," said the widow. " I wish you
had gone two hours ago ; but now it is too late.
Hark ! isn't there some one ? "

Susie ran eagerly to the front door. But the
comer was not Martin. It was Mr. Hiram Hobart,
one of the widow's lodgers.

" O Mr. Hobart ! " said Susie, " I wish you would
come in and see my aunt · she is in great trouble
about something."

Hiram was a shy young man ; and he blushed

and stammered as he entered the widow's sitting-room. But he had a warm and sympathetic heart, and he quite forgot his shyness when he found that he might do something to relieve the widow's distress.

He hurried out again to look for Martin. And now once more Susie and her aunt waited for news of the missing one.

It was almost ten o'clock when Hiram returned from a fruitless search. The jewellers' shops had long been closed. He had walked the streets in vain, looking for Martin. There seemed to be really nothing he could do ; so he had come back, hoping to find the boy at home before him.

But Martin had not come; and he did not appear that night. If he had indeed fallen into temptation and stolen the money, he would certainly have been driven by remorse to hasten home with it if he could have known what agonies of anxiety his kind benefactress was suffering on his account.

"It isn't the money," she said — though that was so much to her — " but to think that he couldn't be trusted ; that's what breaks my heart !"

"Do go to bed and sleep," Susie entreated.

It was now past midnight, and Mr. Hobart had long since gone up to his room.

"Sleep !" said her aunt bitterly, "there's no sleep for me this night. O Martin! Martin !"

"I trust him yet !" Susie declared. "Something

keeps him.   We shall hear from him in the morning."

Indeed, at about ten o'clock the next forenoon news — strange and startling news it was — reached them regarding the lost boy.   In order to explain what it was, we must go back a little.

CHAPTER II

"GIVE ME BACK MY RING"

MARTIN had started off, full of zeal and fidelity, to do his aunt's errand. Walking the street, he kept his hand on the pocket that held the little jewel-case that contained the ring.

He went first to a well-known jewelry-store, which his aunt had recommended ; but the proprietors had gone home, and the clerk told him to come again in the morning.

Then he tried two or three other places, but without success. Then he entered a small shop that showed piles of gold and silver and paper money in the window, together with watches and jewelry, and the notice — "MONEY TO LOAN."

The shop-keeper — a large, dark man, with a coarse mouth and a big nose — examined the jewel, and asked Martin what he considered it was worth.

"Sixty dollars," said Martin stoutly.

The big-nosed man made no reply, but coolly handed the case back over the counter.

"Don't you want it ?" Martin asked.

"Not at that price," said the man with a look of cold indifference.

"What do *you* think it's worth?" Martin insisted.

The man made no reply, but turned to another customer. And now Martin discovered to his alarm that he was in the shop of a pawn-broker, which he accordingly quitted in haste, without waiting for an answer to his question.

He next entered a narrow but elegant shop, where he was politely received by a young salesman.

"Have you a right to dispose of this ring?" said the young man, eying first the jewel, then looking sharply at Martin.

"You will see that I have," the boy replied, showing Mrs. Tolley's card.

"Oh!" the young man smiled. "You consider it a valuable ring?"

"I believe the real worth of it is about sixty dollars."

"Oh!" the young man smiled again, and took the ring to the rear of the shop, where he examined it carefully by a brilliant gaslight. "You haven't found it easy to get that for it, I fancy."

Martin confessed that he had met with difficulties.

"You have offered it in several places?"

"Yes; four or five," Martin stated frankly. "But everybody seemed to think it a valuable ring, except the pawn-broker on Court Street."

"Oh! You offered it to him?"

"Yes; but I didn't like him, and didn't wait to hear what he thought of it."

The young man was so friendly, and seemed to take so much interest in the ring, that Martin had strong hopes that he would buy it. He was greatly disappointed, therefore, when, with another obliging smile, the jewel-case was clasped and handed back to him.

"You can't give me anything on it?" Martin inquired.

"I don't think we could agree about the price," said the young man. "Besides, the boss is away, and I couldn't buy it without his sanction."

"Then why did you look at it and keep me waiting so long?" cried the boy indignantly.

"Why, because you wanted me to look at it, didn't you?" the young man replied blandly.

Martin was going, when, having opened the case, to take a look at the jewel, he started, examined it hurriedly, with a frightened air, and turned upon the salesman.

"This is not my ring! Where is my ring?" he demanded, in accents of despair and terror.

"That is your ring — the ring that was in the case when you gave it to me."

"It is not! You have changed it! Give me back my ring!" And Martin sprang at the young man, who, smiling still, but with an excited face, retreated beyond his reach.

Just then a young fellow with a cigar in his mouth sauntered into the shop. "Hello, Lorton!" he said, "What's the row?"

"I don't know," said the salesman, with some agitation. "This boy says " —

"He does know too!" Martin broke in wildly, appealing to the new-comer. "I showed him a ring in this case. He spent a long time looking at it and talking about it, and when he gave me back the case it had *this* ring in it!"

"Isn't it the same?"

"No! That was a diamond, worth sixty dollars!"

"And how do you know but what this is a diamond worth a hundred dollars?" said the young fellow with the cigar, looking sarcastically at the case which Martin held open.

"Whether it is or not, it is not mine; it is not the ring I gave him. He is trying to rob me, but he sha'n't!" said Martin desperately. "I'll never leave this store till I have my ring — Mrs. Tolley's ring, that I brought here to sell for her, as you will see by this card."

"I don't care anything about your card," said the young fellow, puffing his smoke in Martin's face. "When you accuse Tom Lorton of trying to rob you, it's amusing! What are the facts, Tom?"

"I'll tell you if he'll hold his tongue a minute," said Lorton. "This boy comes to me with a ring in that case, which he wants me to look at. He calls it worth sixty dollars. I don't see any sixty dollars in it; and I give it back to him. Then he roars out that it isn't the same ring."

"You would roar — anybody would roar — robbed

in this way!" Martin again broke in, loudly and furiously.

"It's a little swindle," remarked the young fellow with the cigar.

"I don't know whether it's a swindle," said Lorton, "or whether somebody else changed the ring in the case before he brought to me. He said himself he had been to half-a-dozen places with it; to Carsino's, on Court Street, for one. I'm glad you came in just now, Jim."

"So am I," said Jim. "I don't believe Carsino, or any other man, stole his ring. Say the word, Tom, and I'll hustle him out."

"Don't do that!" cried Martin, with a dangerous fire in his eyes. "It *is* a swindle; but I am the one swindled. Carsino didn't steal my ring, I know, for I kept my eye on him every minute, and he didn't have a chance."

"Will you hush up and clear out?" said Jim, taking Martin by the collar.

"No!" exclaimed Martin fiercely. "I'll never leave this shop till I have back my ring! I'll call for help!" and in his desperation, he rushed to the door and shouted, —

"Robbers! help! police!"

Thereupon Jim stood in the door with him, and drowned his voice, shouting in a still louder key, —

"Police! police!"

CHAPTER III

ALONE IN A NARROW CELL

A POLICEMAN came hurrying to the spot. He hushed the boy, who tried to get in his story, and listened to Jim, as a disinterested witness in the case. Then he heard Lorton's statement, but paid very little heed to Martin's.

"You don't give me any chance!" said Martin, with tears of rage and distress.

"No, we don't give such chaps as you a chance," the policeman replied. "Move on! You've made disturbance enough for one evening."

"I can't move on till I get my ring — Mrs. Tolley's ring!" said Martin imploringly. "Search him; search his boxes and drawers back there, and you'll find a diamond ring with '*F. T.*' engraved on the inside of it!"

"Move on, I tell you!" and the policeman turned Martin's face toward the door. Martin struggled. The policeman seized him roughly. Martin kicked and screamed.

The little jewel-case fell on the ground. Lorton picked it up and started back with it into the shop.

"I'll take that!" cried the officer; and Lorton, pale and excited, gave it up.

"Now come along quietly, or I'll give you a little tap on the head," said the officer, showing his billy, while he dragged his captive away.

"Little rascal!" said Jim, laughing, as he puffed his cigar.

"I don't know!" replied Lorton, gazing after Martin with a troubled face. "The ring *might* have been changed, you know, before he brought it to me."

"A man must be a fool, as well as a scoundrel, to do such a thing as that," said Jim. "Carsino is a sharper, but he wouldn't commit a bare-faced robbery that might be proved against him, and put him in a prison jacket; not he!"

"I should *think* not!" said Lorton, fingering his necktie.

"Why, how pale you are!" said his friend. "Good gracious! how your hand trembles!"

"It's a mighty disagreeable thing to have happen to a fellow, you know!" replied Lorton.

Martin, in the meanwhile, was marched off to a police-station and locked up. In vain he entreated that Mrs. Tolley might be sent for; in vain he tried to interest the officers at the station in his cause.

"You'll have a chance to be heard to-morrow," was all the consolation he received, and he found himself alone in a narrow cell.

He tried to be calm; he tried to think dispassionately of the wrong he had suffered, and of his situation.

It all seemed like a horrible dream to him; and in his bewilderment he began to wonder whether anybody was to blame but himself.

"I was a fool to make such a row," he said, sitting on his bunk, in the dim light that came in through the grated door. "Maybe Lorton *did* give me back the ring I gave him. Carsino, or somebody else, may have changed it by some sleight of hand. I don't know; I can't remember; I can't think!"

His brain was all in a whirl. The one thing that seemed certain was, that he had failed most miserably in doing Aunt Abby Tolley's errand, and lost not only the ring but her good graces forever.

"How can she believe in me again?" he asked himself. "How can she trust me in the slightest thing?"

He remembered how remiss he had often been in his duties; repaying her kindness with ingratitude and neglect. After being to blame in so many things, how would it profit him that he was not to blame in this?

"She will be sure to think I was careless; or" — a dreadful doubt suggested itself — "maybe she will believe *I* stole her diamond!"

Tired out at last, he lay down in his bunk. But his wretched thoughts kept him awake for a long while; and then, just as he was sinking into a feverish slumber, he was awakened by the noise made by a drunken man brought into the station.

All his misery came back upon him in a great

wave. "It must be midnight," he thought. "I wonder if Aunt Abby is sitting up for me. And Susie — what does she think?"

He forgot his troubles at last; and was in a sound sleep the next morning when he was roused by a hand shaking him, and a voice saying, —

"Come, youngster! it's time to be moving."

He started up; stared half-awake at the strange objects surrounding him; and then remembering too quickly where he was and what had brought him there, said beseechingly to the officer, —

"Can I go?"

"Go? yes," was the reply; "that's what we want you to do."

"Home?" said Martin.

"No; to the Tombs," said the officer.

CHAPTER IV

"PRETTY COMPANY I AM IN"

AT the Tombs — the prison under the court-house — he was placed in another dismal cell, and given a dish of coffee and a thick piece of bread, which he ate from very faintness.

Afterwards he was marched with other prisoners through narrow passages which led to the prisoners' dock in the court-room, where he sat on a bench, between a boy of his own age and a gray-haired man of sixty, while some business was going on of which he did not understand a word.

"What are you here for?" he at length whispered to the boy beside him.

"Larceny," said the boy stolidly.

An officer reached over and touched them; and after that there was no more communication between them.

The old man was arraigned for drunkenness.

"Pretty company I am in!" thought the wretched Martin, casting his eyes around upon the other criminals.

The case of the old man was quickly disposed of. Martin's was the next called.

He stood trembling at the bar, while the officer who had arrested him took the witness's oath, and in a brief, business-like way gave his evidence.

The judge stopped writing, and looked over his glasses at the youthful prisoner.

" What is your name ? "

"Martin Gower," said the boy, in a firm, clear voice which surprised himself.

Somehow he was not so frightened as he had thought he would be. Something in the judge's manner gave him courage. Perhaps he would have justice done him.

" Where do you live ? "

"With Mrs. Tolley, on Myrtle Street."

The judge took off his glasses, and holding them between his hands, resting before him on the desk, said gravely, —

" You are charged with disorderly conduct in a jewelry store, and with resistance to the officer who removed you. Have you anything to say for your-self ? "

Poor Martin had so much to say that he merely gasped.

" You heard the evidence," the judge went on ; "were you aware that you were resisting an officer, when you refused to be removed ? "

" I knew he was an officer," said Martin, " but I didn't want to be removed. I had been robbed, and I wanted to get back my ring."

" Isn't that your ring ? " asked the judge, showing

the jewel-case, which the officer had brought into court.

"No, sir," Martin replied firmly. "The case is the one I had my ring in; but the ring was taken out by the young man in the store, and this one was put in its place."

The judge regarded the youthful prisoner with increasing interest.

"Swear him!" he said to the clerk of the court.

Martin took the solemn oath, to tell "the truth, the whole truth, and nothing but the truth;" and, allowed to go on in his own way, told in an earnest, straightforward, convincing manner, the whole story.

"So you did make a disturbance?" said the judge.

"I did! for I felt that I'd rather die than leave that store without the diamond ring my aunt had put in my care," said Martin, his voice breaking, and his eyes glistening with honest feeling.

"You say you had offered the ring in other places; how do you know that it hadn't been changed before?"

Martin had thought the matter all over, and his mind was now clear on that point.

"It couldn't have been. It was hardly out of my hands — never a moment out of my sight — till I offered it to Mr. Lorton. Mr. Carsino had it; but he stood within a yard of me while he looked at it, and I watched him all the while. Mr. Lorton kept it so long that something made me open the case when he gave it back to me ; and it didn't take half a glance to see that he hadn't given me the right ring. "

"What was the difference you noticed?"

" The rings are a good deal alike ; though this has a brighter, newer look than Aunt Abby's ; and there is more of this sort of work on it," said Martin, showing the enchased part of the gold. " But the stone doesn't sparkle like hers. When I saw this I was frightened, and looked for the initials."

"What initials?"

"Her ring has '*F. T.*' engraved on the inside. This ring, you see, has no letters. It didn't take me long," said Martin, "to find all that out. Then I made a row."

" No wonder!" said the judge, "if your story is true. You shall have a chance to verify it ; and this court," he added, sternly, "will do all in its power to render justice in the case. Would you like to call any witnesses ?"

Martin was thrilled with joy.

"I should like to have my aunt sent for," he said. "And some of the jewellers I offered the ring to. Mr. Carsino, at any rate."

"And Thomas Lorton," said the judge curtly. "He should have something interesting to say."

CHAPTER V

"TOM, YOU'RE IN A SCRAPE"

AT that moment a person who had remained partly concealed in the rear of the crowd of spectators slipped out, and hurried away. It was Lorton's young friend, Jim. Not many minutes later, Tom saw him coming into the store. He had been looking for him, and he greeted him with a sickly smile.

"There's an officer coming for you," said Jim in a whisper, over the counter. "If you *did* play that boy a trick, Tom, you're in a scrape!"

The smile grew ghastly, and Tom steadied his arms on the counter. "What's up?" he asked anxiously.

Jim had not for a moment doubted Lorton's innocence the night before. But Martin's straightforward story in the court-room had produced a strong impression on his mind, which now Tom's guilty looks confirmed. He told what had occurred and added, looking his friend searchingly in the eye, —

"Tom, you'd better tell me all about it. Maybe I can help you through. Have you got that boy's ring?"

Tom was frightened. He dropped his eyes and faltered, " No," with pale lips. "I wish I had!"

"What did you do with it?" Jim demanded. And the wretch replied, —

" I — gave — it — away !"

"Oh, you idiot!" Jim exclaimed.

" Yes," said Tom, through his closed teeth, " I've been the biggest confounded idiot under heaven! And it's all owing to that girl!"

Jim was amazed. "Eliza?" he said.

Tom nodded.

"She don't care that for you!" Jim snapped his fingers. " Why did you give it to her?"

"I don't know," Lorton replied bitterly. " She is always teasing me for presents. And I wanted to get that ring off my hands, you know."

While this talk was going on, there was nobody in the shop but a watchmaker at work by the window. But now a customer entered, whom Lorton, masking his terrible anxiety with an obliging smile, turned to wait upon.

Then, before he could resume his conference with Jim, an officer came with the expected summons.

"Wanted as a witness, am I?" said Tom, feigning surprise. "Oh yes! that little affair of last night. All right! I'll come right along."

But just as he was going out with his friend, they met an old gentleman coming in. It was Avery, the proprietor of the shop.

" Where now?" he asked.

Tom had already taken the precaution to tell him something of what had happened the night before. He now reminded him of it in a careless way, adding, "They've got the boy up in court, and I'm wanted as a witness."

He was anxious to get off and continue his talk with Jim. But the old gentleman remarked quietly, —

"I'll go along with you."

Tom did not like that; but there was no help for it, and he went off to court with the old gentleman, talking pleasantly, with a horrible fear at heart.

CHAPTER VI

MORE WITNESSES

AUNT ABBY was watching at the window again that morning, when the officer came to summon her.

Susie ran to open the door, and in her eagerness cried out, almost before the man had opened his mouth, —

"You have news of Martin! Is it good news?"

"I don't know just what you would call it," he replied good-naturedly, and gave a brief account of the boy's situation.

Susie was overjoyed to find that it was no worse. She ran in to her aunt, followed by the officer.

"I told you so!" she cried. "Martin is all right! But the ring has got him into some sort of trouble."

The officer politely removed his hat, took from the breast of his coat a long pocket-book, and from the pocket-book a paper, which he handed to the widow. It was the summons of the court.

That dreadful night of suspense and anxiety had left her almost too weak to bear the shock. But, after all, bad news was better than none; and a few unofficial words from the man, who evidently took an interest in the case, gave her fresh hope and courage.

She was on her lame foot in a moment, too much excited, however, to know just what she was about.

"Why, Aunt Abby!" said Susie, "you can't go to court without your things on! And you can't walk so far, either. Perhaps you think you are going to fly?"

"I can walk!" said the widow, all in a flutter "I don't care so much for the ring, since Martin has proved true. The poor boy! how he must have suffered!"

As no carriage had come for her with the summons, Susie went out to call one, when a grocer's wagon appeared, driven by a lad she knew. He had already heard of Martin's disappearance, and he stopped to ask the news.

"Wait three minutes," he said, after she had told him; "I'm coming back this way, and I'll carry the old lady over."

"Me too," said Susie, "for I am going with her."

"The more the merrier," said the young grocer, whipping up his horse.

He returned as he had promised, and Susie and her aunt mounted to the seat.

Martin had not been formally discharged, but he was no longer treated like a prisoner. He was in the witnesses' box, waiting for his case to be recalled, when, to his unspeakable delight, he saw Aunt Abby hobble into the court leaning on Susie's arm.

Carsino had already arrived, and was waiting inside in the bar. And by the time the case then before

"AUNT ABBIE WAS CALLED TO THE WITNESS STAND." — Page 59.

the court was disposed of, two other witnesses had come in. One of these was Thomas Lorton, accompanied by Mr. Avery.

Aunt Abby was called to the witness-stand. Owing to her lameness, a chair was placed for her; and in a low, tremulous voice, she gave her testimony.

" Your name ? " said the judge.

" Abigail Tolley."

" You reside in Myrtle Street ? "

" Yes, sir," and she gave the number.

" Do you know Martin Gower ? "

" I should think I ought to ! He lives with me."

" When did you part with him last ? "

" Yesterday afternoon, when I sent him out to do an errand."

" What was the errand ? "

" To get some money by selling or pledging a ring."

" Was the ring valuable ? "

" Quite so ; it was a diamond."

" Did you think him a boy to be trusted in a matter of such importance ? "

" I did ! Long as he has lived with me," said the widow, raising her voice, " I have never had the slightest cause to suspect his honesty. Martin is a thoroughly upright, good boy ! "

Tears rushed to the boy's eyes as he heard this, and he could hardly repress a sob. He did not feel that he deserved to have her speak so well of him.

The ring was then shown the witness, and she was asked if she recognized it.

With trembling fingers she put on her spectacles.

"No, sir," she replied. "That looks like the case, but that is not my ring;" and she described the most noticeable points of difference, corroborating Martin's story in every particular.

"That is all," said the judge, and she hobbled back to the witnesses' box.

"Frederick H. Maxwell!" called the clerk.

A gentleman stepped forward whom Martin recognized as one of the jewellers to whom he had offered the ring. The officer had had no difficulty in finding him, by making inquiries at one of the stores Martin described.

He remembered the boy who showed him the ring; the time,—between half-past five and six o'clock the evening before,—and he thought he might identify the ring if he saw it.

"Is that it?" asked the judge.

"No; the stone was a diamond; this is only an imitation."

Carsino was the next witness.

He had not a prepossessing face; but he gave his testimony in a plain, candid, matter-of-fact way, which was very convincing.

He, too, remembered the boy and his ring, and the time when he saw them—about a quarter before six. The ring in the case being shown him, he swore positively that it was not the same.

"This stone is nothing but paste," he said, putting it aside.

"But the stone the boy offered you was a diamond?"

"Oh yes ; a very good stone."

"Then why did you treat it slightingly?" said the judge, referring to that part of the boy's story — the very part, in fact, which favored the idea of Lorton's innocence.

"In the way of business," replied the witness coolly. "I thought he would stay around and finally take a low price for it. But when I looked for him again, he was gone."

"That is all, Mr. Carsino."

And the money-lender stepped down.

"Thomas Lorton!"

CHAPTER VII

TOM LORTON ON THE STAND

SMILING, and very much at his ease, Tom took the stand.

Thomas Lorton — let it here be said — was not by nature a rogue. He belonged to a good family, which up to this time had no stain on its name. He had left his country home at the age of eighteen, to accept a place which his friends had found for him in Avery's jewelry store. For a time he was sober, diligent, and faithful. But it was not long before he fell under the influence of bad companions, and began a course of foolish dissipation. He wasted his nights, his health, and his means.

He ran into debt, and "borrowed" money from his employer's till. He also helped himself occasionally to a jewel to make a present of, for he had the reputation of being a generous fellow. It is so easy to be generous with other people's means !

Tom was very cautious, however, about his petty pilferings from the store. He was determined they should never be found out ; and at first he had really meant to repay the till for everything he took, at some more convenient season.

But that season never came. After the first wrong doing, each downward step came easy to him, until the once amiable and upright youth was prepared for the desperate venture to which he was tempted by Aunt Abby's ring.

It seemed a safe venture. His first impression was that the boy must have stolen so valuable a diamond. Then, why not get possession of it? It certainly could not be a very wrong thing to rob a robber. Lorton even whispered something to his conscience about restoring it to its rightful owner.

In this way his mind was opened to the temptation. Then, when he found that Martin probably had a right to dispose of the ring, he could not abandon the alluring plot which had rapidly shaped itself in his thoughts.

He could put his hand on a ring in the store, which looked so much like this one! Would an unsuspicious boy, who knew nothing of jewelry, be apt to discover the difference?

Then Martin himself innocently encouraged the fraud by confessing that the ring had been offered in other places that night. Even Carsino, who was commonly believed to be a sharper, had had the handling of it. How, then, would it ever be known that it had not been changed before it reached Tom Lorton?

The thing had not worked just as Tom expected. Martin was too quick and shrewd for him. The disturbance which followed alarmed him, and roused, it is to be hoped, some feeling of remorse in his breast.

At any rate, when in the scuffle with the policeman Martin dropped the case, Tom picked it up with the intention of putting the real diamond back into it.

But the officer, as we have seen, prevented him from doing that, and carried away the case with the false ring. Thus, in spite of his better impulse at the last moment, Lorton's crime was complete.

He had been surprised into making a confidant of Jim; but Jim had not helped him. And nothing seemed left for him now to do but to harden his heart and put on a brazen face. When called to the stand, he had had time to make up his mind for the ordeal before him, and was prepared to tell a stout story.

After a few preliminary questions, came this one, —

" Did you take the ring into your hands which the boy showed you?"

"I took the case in my hands, and — yes," said the witness smilingly, " I lifted up the ring enough to look at it."

"How long did you have it?"

"Oh, a few seconds; just long enough to see what it was like."

"Then what did you do?"

" I gave it back to him."

" Did you take it to the rear of the store, and examine it there?"

" I did not," said Thomas Lorton emphatically.

" Please look at the ring in the case, and see if you recognize it."

Thomas examined the ring, and said it resembled very much the one offered him by the boy. But he could not swear to it. He could only swear that he gave back the ring that was shown him.

" Have you rings like that in your store ? "

" I think it very likely; we have almost everything."

" But you cannot say that you have just that class of goods ? "

Thomas was not positive about that; neither was his memory clear as to the time when the boy called on him.

" What reason had you to suppose he was a swindler ? "

" When a person offers me a cheap stone, which he wishes to sell for a diamond, I naturally suspect him," said the witness blandly.

" But would not a swindler, after such an attempt, be more apt to go quietly away, than to attract attention by a great outcry ? "

Lorton was very pale; and his fingers shook so that he took them from the rail before him and put them under his coat-tails. But he was still smiling, though somewhat glassily.

" Perhaps he thought I would give something to hush him up. For, innocent as a man may be, he don't like to have such things happen to him. Or," said Lorton, ready to add wrong to wrong, in order to protect himself, "he might first have stolen the ring entrusted to him, put another in its place, and then made a row about it, to hide his own guilt and throw suspicion upon others."

He had carefully considered this point beforehand ; and it evidently made a strong impression. Many eyes turned upon Martin, who flushed very red, and gave an angry start.

"That is all," said the judge.

And Thomas, feeling that he had got through the examination very well, stepped down with a triumphant smile.

He must have been a little startled, however, when the name of the next witness was called.

"Charles Avery !"

CHAPTER VIII

"OF MORE VALUE THAN MANY RINGS"

THE proprietor of the shop had not been sum-
moned; but his presence in the court had become
known to the judge, who now had an important question to put to him.

"Mr. Avery, please examine the ring in that case.
Did you ever see it before?"

The jeweller looked grave, and hesitated.

"I cannot swear that I ever saw *it* before," he said
at length.

"Have you similar rings in your store?"

"Quite similar."

"You deal in that class of goods?"

And, being pressed, the witness admitted that they
were specially in his line.

The triumphant smile had faded from Thomas
Lorton's face when his employer left the stand.

In reviewing the facts in the case, the judge said, —

"The ring was seen in the boy Gower's hands by
Mr. Maxwell between half-past five and six o'clock.
It was offered to Carsino at a quarter before six.
The witness Lorton could not fix the time when
Gower called on him; but the arrest was made,

according to the officer's statement, a little before
six o'clock.

" It would then appear that the defendant must have
gone pretty directly from Carsino's place to Avery's.
What had he done with the ring in the meanwhile?
Could he, in the few minutes which intervened, have
had time to negotiate it at any other place?

" He is positive that he carried it in the case to
Avery's, and I see no reason for doubting his story.
There is no evidence of any attempt at a swindle —
on his part.

" If his character were bad, and he had had ample
time and opportunity, he might perhaps be suspected
of filching the diamond ring himself, and then of trying to cover his guilt by the ingenious trick suggested
by our witness.   But all the evidence is against such
a supposition."

Martin's face brightened; he looked as if he could
have hugged the court.

"The boy swears that he offered the diamond ring
to Lorton; who gave him back, shut up in the case,
the cheap jewel produced here in court.   Lorton
denies this.   He does not even recognize the cheap
ring as belonging to a class of goods sold in his
employer's store.   But Mr. Avery recognizes at once
if not that particular ring, at least a class of goods
which are specially in his line."

In conclusion the judge said, —

" The defendant, Gower, can hardly be blamed for
making a disturbance in Avery's store, under the cir-

cumstances, or even for objecting pretty strongly to being removed by an officer ; and the court orders his discharge.

"At the same time, the witness Lorton has failed to answer satisfactorily the complaint against him ; a suspicion rests upon him, which needs to be cleared up ; and the court orders his arrest."

So it happened that Thomas Lorton was taken into custody ; while Martin was free to depart with Susie and Aunt Abby.

A time was appointed for the further examination of Lorton ; and he was admitted to bail, Mr. Avery becoming his surety. The court then adjourned.

Susie was in great glee at this result ; and Martin's satisfaction was marred only by the loss of the ring. Aunt Abby bewailed that, of course ; but looking affectionately at Martin, after he and Susie had taken her home, she said,—

"But *you* were not to blame, my dear ; and a boy's good name is of more value than many rings."

Martin felt how true that was. His eyes filled with tears.

"Aunt Abby," he said, "I've had a chance to think things over a little ; I know I haven't always done by you as I should, after what you have done for me ; but now I'm going to deserve the good name you gave me in court to-day — I am, Aunt Abby!"

"And I'm sure you will, my dear boy!" said Aunt Abby, putting her arm about him ; while Susie cried for sympathy, looking on.

CHAPTER IX

"I HAVE YOU TO THANK"

THE history of the diamond ring had a curious termination.

The postman brought to the house that afternoon two letters. One was from Luther, who made haste to announce the good news that he had sold half his patent for a handsome sum, and that he no longer needed money.

The other turned out to be no letter at all. It was only an envelope containing, carefully wrapped up in blank paper, Aunt Abby's diamond ring!

Perhaps this was the reason of the case against Lorton being dropped. Martin never saw him again ; but two years later a gentleman came into the express-office where he was then at work, and offered him his hand.

"You have the advantage of me," said Martin.

"My name is Warner," said the stranger. "Don't you remember Tom Lorton's friend Jim ?"

"I do!" cried Martin, "very well, indeed."

"I did you great injustice once," said Jim. "But it was all owing to my faith in that fellow. I couldn't believe he was such a fraud ! "

"What has become of him?" Martin inquired.

"He left Avery's very soon after his affair with you; he couldn't stand the disgrace it brought upon him. I last heard of him leading a sort of hand-to-mouth life in California. 'Twas a great pity he should have gone to the bad, in the way he did!"

"I'm grateful to him for one thing," said Martin. "He sent back Aunt Abby's ring."

Jim laughed. "No, he didn't."

"Who did, then?"

"I did. He had put it out of his hands. I found out the girl he had given it to, went to her, frightened her, got the ring, and sent it in an envelope to Mrs. Tolley."

"Then I have *you* to thank!" Martin exclaimed.

"Not much," said Jim. "For I am more indebted to you than you think. I was going the same way with poor Tom, when that affair opened my eyes to the danger, and I turned square about."

Martin gave him his hand again. And from that time the two were fast friends.

LOST ON THE TIDE

CHAPTER I

AT THE MOUTH OF KENNEBUNK RIVER

The Kennebunk River flows into the sea between two long granite breakwaters, or piers, which ward off the sand-bars and keep the channel open.

Outside is the ocean, forever changing in sun and breeze and storm ; within is a small, safe harbor for yachts and coasters and fishing-boats, in a broadening of the stream which becomes at high tide a way for steamers and ships.

I said the river flows into the sea. I might have said, the sea flows into the river. Twice every day and night the tides come rushing impetuously in, flooding the broad clam-beds, brimming the sandy beaches, and overflowing the borders of the grassy flats, sometimes the flats themselves ; then rushing out again as swiftly on their wild, mysterious errands.

Near the mouth of the river are Ocean Bluff and Cape Arundel, delightful summer resorts, with their evergreen woods, berry-fields, long shining beaches,

73

and sea-buffeted rocks. It was here that Mrs. Paul
Barden went to board, not many summers ago, in a
cottage by the river, with her two boys and their
Aunt Ann.

It was a fine place, especially for the boys. Paul
was thirteen years old, and Tommy six. Mrs. Barden
was a nervous invalid, and Aunt Ann had the care of
her. Mr. Barden ran down from Boston only once
in a while to spend a Sunday with his family. So it
happened that the boys were left very much to
themselves.

They liked that. Playing in the sand by the river
or on the sea-beach; fishing from the wharf before
their door or from the long granite pier; boating,
bathing, berrying, or watching the yachts and schoon-
ers as they entered or left the river, often baffled by
wind and tide; then launching their own little ships
with paper sails; there were never two happier boys
by the sea, where boys, I believe, are always
happy.

And Paul took excellent care of his little brother.
He managed somehow to have him with him wherever he went. Tommy was a brave little fellow,
eager for every adventure; and he would never own
that he was tired, until he would sometimes lie down
on the rocks, or among the blueberry bushes, and
fall asleep.

They had the use of a boat, and nothing Paul liked
better than to row up to the village and back again
with the tide. He had done this one evening after

supper, and had a fine time, with the added pleasure of bringing home a letter from his father. How proud and glad both boys were to have made their mother so happy !

Two evenings later they got Aunt Ann's permis-sion to try the same thing over again. Aunt Ann had learned to trust Paul in almost everything ; and she did not know much about the tides.

CHAPTER II

"A TUSSLE WITH THE TIDE"

BUT the tide was later this evening by nearly two hours. Paul himself had not fully considered that. It was, besides, about the time of the full moon, when the tides usually run very high. And a strong wind from the sea united with the attraction of the sun and moon in heaping up the waters.

The tide was so well up that Paul thought it would turn in half an hour, when, in the cool twilight, he pushed off his dory, with his little brother seated in the stern, sprang to the oars, and gleefully rowed out into the swift current.

Past the wharf ; past the little harbor where the yachts and fishing-boats lay; past the flats which were fast becoming flooded ; between the cool green shores, the boat shot with the speed imparted to it by wind and tide and oars, — though the oars had little to do but to keep it in mid-stream.

The boys laughed and shouted with excitement.

"Now, if we only get another letter from father ! " cried Paul. "He said he would write again in two days, to let us know if he would be coming down here to-morrow."

They did get the letter, and ran back with it joyfully to the village wharf, where they had fastened their boat.

"Oh what a tide!" Paul exclaimed. "It's running like a race-horse yet, and there's no sign of its turning."

"You can't pull against it; we shall have to wait," said little Tommy, repeating what he had heard his brother say at other times.

"But we can't wait; this wharf will be nearly under water in a little while at this rate," Paul answered. "Besides, there's a fog blowing in, and we sha'n't see any moon to-night."

"I'm not afraid!" said Tommy, taking his seat in the stern.

"Of course not!" And Paul pushed boldly off, turning his dory in the tranquil eddy between the wharves. "The tide *must* turn before long, and we can get home before it's very dark, anyway."

"Aunt Ann won't care," said Tommy.

"No. But I don't want to make mother sick!" Paul replied. "I think I can work my way back, if I keep out of the current, along by the shores."

So sure he was of being able to do this, that it did not occur to him that they might better leave their dory at the wharf and walk home. It was only a mile by the river-road.

"I'm not afraid of a tussle with the tide!" cried Paul, pulling with all his might to get his dory around the end of the next wharf.

The tussle had begun. How fast the oars flew! how the water splashed !

"I don't care if you do spatter me!" said heroic little Tommy, from his seat in the stern.

Paul was too breathless to speak. The current was powerful around the end of the wharf. It actually carried the dory back with it for a few seconds. Then Paul, by putting forth all his boyish strength, began to make headway against it.

Slowly! but the pull was a short one; and after a struggle he found himself in the next eddy.

"I never saw such a tide!" he gasped out, pausing to wipe the sweat from his face. "I'll rest a minute."

He was wise enough to get out on the next wharf and haul the dory around it. After that he had a broad sheet of water to row in, where he could keep out of the strong current.

But, in the windings of the river, the current runs most powerfully, now near one shore, now near the other; and Paul, as he kept on, had often to cross and row against it.

Besides, the wind was blowing hard. Thick clouds and fog rolled in from the sea; and it soon grew so dark that he often got into the swiftest part of the current before seeing where he was.

For a long while nothing was said. Paul was too busy or too scant of breath to talk. Then, as they were traversing a broad spread of the tide, where rowing would have been easy but for the wind, he said cheerily, —

"This letter will be worth reading when mother gets it, won't it, Tommy?"

Tommy made no reply. He had sunk down quietly in the stern of the dory, and his head was on his breast.

"You all right, Tommy?" cried Paul.

Still no answer, — for a very good reason. Tommy was fast asleep.

"Let him sleep!" muttered Paul. "He can't help me any by keeping awake. Some boys would get scared and cry! Anything but a bawling baby in a boat!" And once more he tugged at the oars.

At the end of another twenty minutes he said, "Wake up, now, Tommy. We are almost there!"

But Tommy was in one of his heavy slumbers, from which nothing short of a good shaking could ever rouse him.

"Never mind!" said Paul. "No use of troubling him till I get the boat ashore."

He was now in the little harbor where the yachts were. But to reach the beach where he kept his dory, he had to pass the wharf.

The wharf is built well out into the channel, which is there so narrowed that the tide sweeps by its slimy timbers with tremendous force. Paul found that his worst struggle was to come. Still he might have conquered, if he had not been quite worn out already.

As it was, after pulling a while with all his might, in the fog, against wind and waves, he gave up reaching the sandy shore beyond, and rowed in towards the wharf. The edge of it, owing to the high tide, was under water, so that he could not lay hold of it with his hands. And the current whirled the boat about the moment he stopped rowing.

Holding on to an oar with one hand, he kept the boat near the wharf, while he caught up the painter with the other. Then he dropped the oar and jumped out. What happened next he never quite understood, and he could never explain.

He remembered that he found himself on one of the outer timbers of the wharf. It was slippery, with a rounding edge; and the river was rushing over it. Then, just as he was stepping back to surer footing, wind and tide together gave a sudden tug at the rope in his hands.

Instead of going backwards, he was jerked suddenly forward. To save himself from plunging headlong into the water, he instinctively threw down his hands and made a clutch at the timber.

He did save himself. But what had happened? He had no rope in his hand. And the boat? The boat was gone! The boat, and Tommy still fast asleep in it.

Paul screamed as he saw it shoot away in the fog; scrambled wildly after it; nearly lost his footing again on the partially overflowed wharf; and at last found himself alone, amidst darkness and a noise of rushing wind and waves, with no boat and no little brother in sight.

"THE BOAT WAS GONE." — Page 80.

"Tommy!" he called, as loud as he could.

But no Tommy replied.   He was sleeping soundly through it all; as unconscious of the stream carrying him away as he was of his brother left terror-stricken on the wharf.

CHAPTER III

THE ESCAPED DORY

PAUL ran for help.   But now he stifled his shrieks, thinking, " I mustn't frighten mother ! "

He met a man coming to the wharf.   " O Mr. Abel ! is that you ? " he cried.

Mr. Abel kept the cottage where Mrs. Barden boarded.   " I've been waiting for you, boys," he said. " Your aunt is concerned about you.   But I told her you would get home all right.   Where's Tommy ? "

" Gone ! gone with the boat !   It got away !"   And in a few hurried words the frightened boy told his story.

" Well! I never heard of anything like that ! " was Mr. Abel's comment.   " But don't take on so.   I'll get another boat — somewhere — let me see !   There's boats enough, if I could only get a pair of oars.   Oars are all locked up at this time of night."

" But we must hurry ! before mother knows !" said Paul.

" Of course.   She has gone to bed, I believe.   You had better go and let your aunt know you've got back.   And tell her Tommy is in no danger.   We can find him."

"But if he should wake up, and be frightened!"

"All the better," said Mr. Abel. "Then we shall hear him call."

"But he might tumble overboard!" said Paul.

"We'll hope he won't do that," Mr. Abel answered. "I think I'd better get a lantern. Then I'll see what I can do for oars."

While he was getting ready to start, Paul ran to the door, where he found Aunt Ann waiting for him.

"What made you so long? Why, what has happened? Where is Tommy?"

She uttered question after question, in whispers, before Paul could answer a word. Then he whispered in reply, —

"Tommy is asleep in the boat. The tide is so strong I can't bring it in; but Mr. Abel is going to help me. Here's a letter for mother!" And without giving his aunt any more alarming information, he hastened to rejoin Mr. Abel.

But she followed, and found them in the kitchen. Mr. Abel was explaining the situation to his wife, while he lighted the lantern. "Lucky the tide wasn't running the other way," he said. "It might have carried him right out to sea."

Aunt Ann overheard that. "Who? Tommy?" she demanded. "Has the tide carried him away?"

It wasn't possible to keep the truth from her any longer.

"O Paul!" she said reproachfully. "I thought you such a careful boy! How could you let such a thing happen to your little brother?"

"I don't know! I couldn't help it!" And the poor fellow tried to explain again how it all occurred.

"Your mother won't sleep a wink all night, if she knows," said Aunt Ann. "She can't bear it."

"She needn't know. Take the letter to her, and tell her it is so late — and we got a little wet — you think Tommy and I had better not go in to bid her good-night. We shall certainly find him, sha'n't we, Mr. Abel?" Paul asked in great distress.

"No doubt on't," said Mr. Abel.

"I suppose *I* was to blame for letting them go," said Aunt Ann. "But I didn't know about the tide."

"How long we are starting!" Paul exclaimed. "Can't I be finding some oars?"

"We shall have to borrow Capt. Ball's," said Mr. Abel. "But they are locked up in his back room, and I guess he's abed."

Capt. Ball *was* abed. But he got up quickly; and when he found his neighbor at the door with a lantern and a strange story of a lost boy, he hastened to bring out his oars.

"You can take my dory; and I'll go with you," he said, "if you'll give me a minute to dress."

"Come on!" said Mr. Abel. "We'll be getting the boat off. There's no need of your going, my boy," he said to Paul, as they hastened down to the shore. "You can't do any good."

"But I *must* go!" Paul exclaimed resolutely. "Think I can stop at home while you are hunting up the river for my little brother?"

"Well, you can hold the lantern," said Mr. Abel, "and keep a look-out. Guess your eyes are as sharp as anybody's."

Capt. Ball came tramping after them down to the beach, buttoning his jacket. He had an extra paddle to steer with. Mr. Abel pulled the oars, and Paul with the lantern perched himself on his knees in the bow.

With its circle of light moving before it over the foggy water, the dory glided past the wharf, and entered the lake-like expanse beyond. The little harbor was brimmed, and the flats were flooded. The creeks on each side making into it were like broad rivers.

Shading his eyes with one hand, while he steadied his lantern on the prow with the other, Paul peered with anxious face into the gloom.

CHAPTER IV

THE MIDNIGHT SEARCH

ONLY now and then a word was spoken. The oars clanked in the row-locks, and dripped and splashed as they rose and fell; there was no other sound, except the thundering breakers farther and farther away.

They crossed and recrossed the river, and examined the mouths of the creeks and the jutting points of land; and now and then they called and listened.

But no drifting dory was to be seen, and no lost boy made answer.

"Who would have thought the tide could carry him so far?" said Paul, giving way at length to his discouragement.

"Never mind," said Mr. Abel cheeringly. "We're bound to paddle till we find him."

The night was still foggy, but the wind had died away.

"Often happens so," said Capt. Ball, who was a weather-wise old fisherman. "Wind stops blowing when the tide stops flowing."

"I believe the tide has turned," Mr. Abel said,

poising his oars, and watching the bubbles by the lantern-light.

"Then he'll stop drifting up stream," said Paul. "Oh, where *can* that dory have gone?"

"We might pass it two or three times and not see it," observed Capt. Ball. "That lantern don't give no more glimmer in a big fog than a good smart lightning-bug."

The tide had indeed turned; it was already begin- ning to run the other way.

"He'll be drifting down stream now," Mr. Abel said, "and we can't miss him."

"Without we've missed him already," Capt. Ball replied. "In that case, the tide may carry him out to sea while we're looking for him up here."

That was a terrifying thought to Paul; and Mr. Abel seemed impressed by it.

They had reached the village; but everything was so changed there that it was not easy to tell where they were. The wharves, built far out into the river, were nowhere to be seen; a wide sheet of water covered them. But on the left, the ship- yards, with their huge skeleton hulls, rose ghost-like in the fog as the dory passed.

"Seems to me he can't have gone up above the bridge," said Mr. Abel. "Guess we'd better work our way back."

"Oh, yes!" Paul exclaimed; "before the tide gets to running fast."

He was filled with horror at the thought of his

brother being swept out into the open ocean. They gave a last look up the river. Then the dory, with the hazy star of light at its bow, swung slowly about on the tide.

"I believe I'd better run in and tell my brother," said Mr. Abel, "and get him to help us. He can take his boat and go up the river, while we go down."

"Oh, do!" said Paul, ready to sob, but manfully controlling himself.

"'Twon't do no hurt to have five or six boats out," said Capt. Ball, "if we expect to find the boy before morning. There's no knowing where the currents may have carried him."

That did not tend to cheer up Tommy's brother, you may be sure. But suddenly, as they were moving towards the shore, Paul cried out, —

"There's a dory adrift!"

"Sartin, it looks so," said Capt. Ball. "But 'tain't the cut of your dory, Mr. Abel."

"No, and it isn't adrift," said Mr. Abel, "though it looks so. Hear that?"

His dripping oar touched gravel, though they seemed to be in mid-stream. He was in fact rowing *over* a wharf, to which the discovered dory was fastened.

It took him some time to find a good landing-place. Then it was several minutes before he could run to his brother's house, rouse him up — for he had gone to bed — and engage him in the search.

But at last all this was done; and he hastened back to the boat, where Paul and the captain were waiting.

"My brother will get help and go up the river," he said. "And now, while you take the oars, Captain, and give another good hunt as you row back, I'll keep the road and run down to our wharf, to watch for the dory and see that it don't go out to sea."

"That's the wisest plan yet," said the captain, taking the oars. "Just give us a push-off; and luck to you!"

He pulled away; and once more the boat, with the lantern at its prow, and a trembling anxious boy on the look-out, moved out across the water.

Mr. Abel straggled back to the village street. He was more alarmed at the thought of Tommy drifting out with the tide than he had been willing to let Paul see. As soon as he was sure of his footing he began to run.

It was not so dark but that he could keep the street; and for a while he got on very well. Then he began to stop in splashes of water, which grew deeper and deeper as he kept on.

The village street had become the river-road. It was built across the flats; and it was now overflowed. Mr. Abel was soon in water over his shoes, and in constant danger of walking off into the trenches on each side.

The clouds, or the fog, had thinned a little, and by

the increasing light he could see what a tremendous tide it was that Tommy had been lost on.

He regretted not having left the river-road, and taken the one over the hills. But that was a round-about way ; and he would have lost much time in going back on his course and crossing over to it. So, impeded as his progress was by the water he had to wade through, he thought it best to keep on.

He was thus much longer in reaching the wharf than he had anticipated. The tide was fast going out when he got there ; and the dreadful question rose in his mind, — had the dory already been swept past?

It was not so dark but that he could have seen an object as large as a boat moving between the two shores. He was gazing eagerly across, when Aunt Ann came out to him.

"Is that you, Mr. Abel? Oh!" she exclaimed, as he answered her, "what is the news?"

"Nothing very encouraging," he replied. "I've got two boats hunting up the river ; and I've hurried down here to see that the missing dory don't dodge us, and get out to sea. The next thing is to make sure of catching it if it comes," he said. "I've got an oar, to scull with ; now I must wade out to that boat."

It was a boat that had been left fastened to a stone dropped near the ordinary high-water mark, on the shore below the wharf. But now the stone was covered by at least two feet of water, and the boat was swinging by its painter beyond.

It was soon secured and drawn ashore, and made ready to launch the moment the runaway dory should appear.

" Now somebody must keep a look-out from this spot until that boy is found, if it's all night," said Mr. Abel.

CHAPTER V

"HOW COULD HE BE IN THE MEADOW"

I⊤ had been all Aunt Ann could do during the past half-hour to keep the mother pacified. Mrs. Barden was still ignorant of what had happened; but she seemed to feel the shadow of a coming calamity.

Ann maintained her calmness very well in the invalid's presence. But why was she constantly leaving the room? It was now getting late, and there seemed to be no good reason why she remained so watchful.

"Has anything happened to my boys?" Mrs. Barden at last demanded.

"Why do you ask such a question as that?" Ann replied, as quietly as she could. "Paul was a little wet when he came in. But I've seen them both much wetter."

"I feel that something is not right," the mother insisted. "They might have bid me good-night, if they *were* wet. Go to their room and see if they are sleeping well, then come and tell me."

So poor Ann went out again, feeling that she must soon resort to downright falsehood, or else confess the truth, which she knew would be so perilous to her sister's health. But instead of visiting the boy's chamber, she hastened once more to the river-side where Mr. Abel was keeping his lonely watch.

The tide was flowing and gurgling, the sea was thundering on the beach outside, and she could hear the tramp of Mr. Abel's feet on the gravel as he walked to and fro.

"No news?" she said.

"The fog is lifting; that's news, and good news!" Mr. Abel replied. "If the moon comes out, we can soon find that dory, if it's in the river."

"But if it has gone out to sea!" said Aunt Ann.

"We may still find it, though it won't be so easy a matter. If it drifts around on the shore, it may get swamped in the breakers."

"I shall have to tell his mother; I may as well go and break it to her at once!" Ann exclaimed.

"Wait a few minutes," Mr. Abel said. "The boats are coming. I've seen them for some time; one on the river, and the other up the creek there."

"We must get more help," said Ann. "There is somebody coming."

It was a party of young yachters who had been up at the hotel, and were now returning to their boat.

Mr. Abel hailed them. The story of the lost boy was soon told, and they readily agreed to engage in the search.

The wharf had now emerged from the tide, and Mr. Abel went with them to the upper end of it, where their yacht lay. While they were getting off their small boat, the clouds parted, and the light of the moon shone full upon the scene.

The bay lay like a sheet of dark silver, unruffled by the wind, and broken into ripples only where the current ran. The distant shores were dimly lighted up. How easy it would have been to discover the lost dory with such moonlight, at the start !

The clank of row-locks was heard. A boat was approaching the wharf. Mr. Abel hailed it, and his brother's voice replied. Each asked eagerly for news. The brother had to announce that he had just passed Capt. Ball's boat, and that no discoveries had been made by either.

Mr. Abel called ; and Capt. Ball himself soon rowed down to the wharf. A short consultation ensued ; then Mr. Abel said, —

" The only thing to be done, is to try again. These young men will help. If the moon keeps on shining, we can find that boat in half an hour, if it hasn't gone out to sea, or been caught under a bridge and been swamped by the rising tide."

"This boy had better go home," said Capt. Ball. "He's used up."

"I'm better now," said Paul ; "and I'm going with you ! I can never go back to that house and see my mother, unless I go with Tommy."

It must be owned that he had given up hope and cried a little at one time. But he was resolute now.

The boats set off together, each to pursue a different route. Mr. Abel went with Paul and the old

captain, two of the yachters agreeing to stay and
watch the river for the drifting dory.

It had been thought impossible that it could have
gone up the first creek, on the side of the river-road,
on account of the high tide and the bridge. But it
might have gone over the road, and perhaps have
lodged on the flats.

The yacht's small boat was to search in that direction. Mr. Abel's brother was to explore the next
creek above, while Mr. Abel himself was to follow
the sinuosities of the shores where a large creek
came in on the opposite side.

The mouth of this creek was still a broad basin,
but it was emptying fast. Mr. Abel took the lower
shore, and rowed up as far as it seemed possible the
dory could have been carried ; then turned back, ex-
ploring the other bank.

"That dory ain't nowheres along here, sure's a
gun!" said Capt. Ball. "It's my positive idee it
went out with the tide while we was looking for't, or
rather feeling for't, in the fog."

"Oh, don't give it up!" Paul pleaded despairingly.

But Mr. Abel was himself more than ever of the
captain's opinion. "All is, we must go outside and
search the rest of the night," he said, rowing reluctantly away.

Meanwhile no discoveries had been made by the
other boats ; and between her distress on account of
the lost boy, and her anxiety for the invalid, poor Ann
knew not what to do. She had returned as softly as

possible to the room, hoping that her presence might not be noticed, when Mrs. Barden, who seemed to be resting quietly, started up in bed.

"My boys! You don't tell me about my boys!" she exclaimed, wildly. "Must I get up and go to them myself? Are they safe? Are they well?"

"Do be calm! Try to be strong, please!" Ann entreated, "and I will tell you everything."

The time had come when she must speak; and she could not speak falsely. She tried to soften the truth in the telling; but the mere fact that Tommy was lost on the tide, and that he had probably drifted out to sea in the fog, was too terrible for any words to lighten.

Mrs. Barden sat upright, staring in a sort of paralysis of fright, while Ann made her confession; then, instead of falling back exhausted, put forth sudden, surprising strength.

"What are you going to do?" cried Ann. "You will not get up!"

"I can't stay here," was the reply. "I am going to seek my boy!"

She persisted in that determination, despite all Ann could do; and was partially dressed, when a clatter of feet was heard on the stairs, the door was burst open, and in rushed Paul.

"Where is your brother?" she cried. "The brother who was left in your care?"

She did not reproach him. But he would not have minded if she had. He was radiant.

"I lost him on the tide," he said exultantly; "but I found him in the meadow, and here he is!"

The next moment Tommy was in his mother's arms.

"How could he be in the meadow?"

Aunt Ann laughed and sobbed at the sight.

"How could he be? I'll tell you!" cried Paul. "We had been around the shores of the big creek, and given him up; and we were coming away to look for him out at sea, when I heard a voice. We put back quick, you'd better believe! I jumped ashore, and if I didn't scramble up through the tall wet grass in a hurry, for once, then no matter! The dory was nowhere in sight, but I heard the voice again, —

"'Paul, where are you?'"

"Well, I didn't want to be left all alone out there!" spoke up Tommy complainingly.

"But how did you ever get there?" cried the overjoyed mother.

"Wait and let me tell!" said Paul, motioning Tommy to be silent. "I followed the voice, and it was moonlight; and what do you think I found up there in the meadow, high and dry,— only it wasn't very dry, you fancy! The boat that had been carried up by the tide and left in the deep grass! And Tommy in it, whimpering and rubbing his head, that had been resting on the rail of the boat. Didn't you hear Mr. Abel shout?"

"Guess you'd have whimpered," said Tommy.

"I didn't want to stay all night in that old boat. I was almost asleep."

Thereupon Paul danced with glee. "Almost asleep!" he chuckled. "Why, he had just waked up from the soundest nap he ever had! He had slept through the whole of it, — the fog, and the moonshine, and the rush of the tide, and our shouts, and the roar of the sea, — while we were half dead with fright, looking for him. We brought him off, but left the dory; and there you can see it with your own eyes to-morrow from these windows, if the grass over there isn't high enough to hide it."

It was an hour of extraordinary excitement to the invalid ; but fortunately it did her no harm. On the contrary, the joy of seeing her boy again, so soon after she had heard of his loss, stimulated her with new life.

And when Mr. Barden came down to the seaside the next day, and found the boys safe and the mother so much better, he fondled Tommy, and said, looking across at the meadow, where the dory still lay in sight, —

"After all, it was a bright idea of yours to get lost on the tide!"

SISTER MARSH'S BEAU

CHAPTER I

"A PERFECT GENTLEMAN"

I DISLIKED him (said the major) at first sight. And when he began to pay his respects to my sister Marsh, — her name was Marcia, but we always called her Marsh, — my prejudice got an edge on it that was bound to make things lively for him, in a way he wouldn't like.

It led me, in fact, to do the meanest and most reckless thing that any boy of common honesty and an average amount of brains ever did. I'll tell you how it happened.

I must plead my youth by way of excuse, in the first place. I was only fifteen ; and I offset my very limited knowledge of life by an unlimited amount of self-conceit. That's the compensation kind old nurse Nature grants a fool. The less he knows, the more he thinks he knows. The more ignorance, the more vanity and self-will.

Sister Marsh was a widow, about twice as old as I.

Our parents were dead, and I had neither money nor friends ; and she had taken me into the little home left her by her husband, supporting me and keeping me in school till I should be able to take care of myself.

She wasn't rich, either.   But I remember that she had, besides her house and lot, a deposit of about twelve hundred dollars in the city savings bank. She drew the interest on that regularly, amounting to sixty dollars a year, besides the extra dividend every fifth year ; but she was extremely careful not to touch any part of the principle.

"I must keep that to live on in my old age," she would say ; "for I don't care to go to the poor-house when I get through with vest-making."

She made vests for a tailoring firm in town ; and to meet her expenses, and keep me fed and clothed, she would often sit up half the night at work with her needle, in order not to be obliged to break in upon that sacred twelve hundred in the bank.

I didn't suppose she had any idea of ever marrying again, until that fellow came along.   She had refused two or three good offers ; a most exasperating thing for me to reflect upon, when I saw her ready to throw herself away upon a miserable adventurer.

He was a man about forty years old, a trifle seedy, but most carefully brushed and combed as to his hat and whiskers, and quite too overflowing with smiles and polite flourishes, I thought.

He had appeared as a stranger in the village,

where ne prolonged his stay under various pretences. First, it was to make up his mind as to the amount of land-damages which would have to be paid by a new railroad in which he claimed to be largely interested.

Then he talked about buying up real estate, for an advance in value if the road should be built, though his operations in that line never got beyond the talking stage.

His large and liberal style of conversation and his elaborately fine manners made a buzz in the village, where Sister Marsh chanced to meet him. Then he drove out to call on her, — we lived about a mile and a half from the hotel where he boarded, — pretending that he had heard her place was for sale, and had come to learn the price.

"I never thought of selling," she said, in some surprise.

"Ah, indeed!" he replied. "Excuse me for troubling you. It is a matter I cannot urge, of course ; for though it might be for my interest to buy, I am bound to tell you frankly that it will not be for your interest to sell. Your place, madam, will doubtless be worth double what it is now after our new road gets established."

She thought it wonderfully magnanimous in Mr. Charles Ammidown — for that was the name he went by — to tell her that. He succeeded in interesting her very much in the new railroad, and still more, I am sorry to say, in himself.

" It would have been dishonorable in me," he said,
as he was going away, — hat off, at the door, smiling
and flourishing, — " very dishonorable indeed, to
keep back anything which it may be to your advantage to know. But, madam, if you *should*, after
this, make up your mind to sell, I venture to ask that
you will give me the first chance."

Sister Marsh was radiant. She beamed upon him
from the doorway, and said, " I certainly will! though
after what you tell me, I should decide not to sell at
present, even if I had thought of such a thing
before."

" That's right, that's right, madam," he said. " I
commend your good sense," and bowing again under
his uplifted hat, Mr. Charles Ammidown stepped to
his buggy at the gate and drove away.

In a few days he called again ; thinking, he said,
she might possibly have changed her mind about
parting with the place.

She had not changed her mind ; but she was delighted to see him, and talked with him an hour, blushing red as a rose over her vest-making, and more
than ever charmed by his smiles and promises and
compliments.

Then he made a third visit in order to " post her
up," he said confidentially, " in a matter of great
importance."

He had recommended that a passenger-station
should be built on a site about forty rods from her
house ; and he had no doubt that the railroad company would take his advice.

"That," he said, "will increase the value of your lot at least five or six times, and I thought you ought to know it. Don't sell, madam, at present, for any consideration."

She was extremely grateful for this private information, which she took care not to impart to anybody but me. But, as I tell you, I hated the man by instinct, and even this extraordinary act of generosity failed to conciliate me.

"He's a perfect gentleman!" she said warmly, seeing me inclined to ridicule him.

"He's a perfect humbug!" I replied; "and I hope he will never show that smirking mug of his again in *this* house!"

"That's a pretty way for you to speak of my visitors!" she exclaimed. "It is my house, sir!" — I was always *sir* to her when she was angry with me, — "and if you don't like the company in it, you'd better leave."

Then *I* was nettled. "You can turn me out-doors if you like," I said. "But that won't make me call a bad dollar a good dollar, when I can see plainly enough that it's a counterfeit, and it's going to be passed off on you."

"What do you mean by counterfeit?" says she.

"I mean that your gentleman is pinchbeck. Mr. Chawles Ammidown" — I drawled out the *Chawles* sarcastically — "is bogus. That's what everybody says, except some silly women."

"I'm one of those silly women, I suppose!" she said, with eyes sparkling.

I made no reply.

"Well, sir! who is everybody? Tell me that!"

"Mr. Cole, for one," I replied. "He says he wouldn't give ten cents for Ammidown's interest in the railroad, or in any other honest business."

At that she tossed her head with supreme contempt. As Mr. Cole was a neighboring farmer who had once offered to marry her, and had been refused, she thought it easy to account for *his* prejudice.

"Such a remark comes with a very bad grace from *him*," she said. "He might at least have kept his opinion to himself, instead of trying to turn you against a stranger and a friend of mine.'

She was too much excited to make her language altogether consistent.

"A stranger and a friend of yours! That's good!" I said, with a laugh, and walked out of the house.

After that, Ammidown's visits became so frequent that the boys began to twit me about him.

"He'll put your nose out of joint, Herbert!" they said. "There won't be room in the house for you and him too."

I was beginning to find that out. I had been accustomed to spend very pleasant evenings with Sister Marsh; but he had already occasioned a decided coolness between us, and she treated me with irritating reserve, even when he wasn't present to monopolize her society.

That was a common occurrence. He would ride or stroll over after tea, and I always felt that his walking into the sitting-room was a signal for me to walk out. All that was left for me to do was to mope alone in the kitchen, or go to the village, or go to bed.

If that was the case before she was married, how, I asked myself, would it be afterwards ?

CHAPTER II

"A LITTLE ACCIDENT FOR HIS MAJESTY"

AMMIDOWN must have been aware of my bitter prejudice against him; for after his first two or three visits, he wasted no more politeness on me, but smiled — when he deigned to smile on me at all — in a way which said plainly, "Young man, you'll get your pay when I am master here!"

Now, mind you, I still maintain that in regard to the man's real character, I was mainly in the right. But, unfortunately, I must go and do the foolish thing I set out to tell you about, and put myself in the wrong.

That he was fishing for my sister's little bit of property, proved only too true. Nevertheless, the method I took to get rid of him was characteristic of a boy who had about five times as much head-strong self-will as good sense and prudence.

I took some other boys into my counsel; and one evening after he had given Sister Marsh a ride, when his buggy was left standing at the gate, we prepared a little accident for his majesty. Then, in order that I might not be suspected of having anything to do with it, I stole back into the house and went to bed.

There in the silence and darkness my conscience began to be troubled ; and I said to myself, " Suppose he should be killed ! wouldn't we be his murderers ? " And I blamed Josh Woods for suggesting the trick which I had been only too willing to adopt.

" If it hadn't been for him," I reasoned, " I never should have thought of it." And I concluded that Josh must be a terribly wicked boy.

It is a comfort to have somebody else to blame for our misdeeds. But that did not relieve me of my share of the responsibility, which grew heavier and heavier, as I lay there in the dark, waiting for the accident I had been so eager for beforehand.

"Won't he ever go ? " I said ; for, much as I now dreaded what I knew was coming, I wanted it over with ; I could not endure the torturing suspense.

Then a desperate impulse seized me. It might not be too late to prevent the catastrophe ; and I was on the point of getting up and going out to find Josh, in order to undo our mischief, when the sound of voices moving towards the front door, from the sitting-room under my garret, warned me that Ammidown was taking leave.

They stopped in the entry to talk two or three minutes longer, with a cheerfulness which was in ghastly contrast with the state of my own mind as I lay and listened.

" How little she dreams of the trap we have set for him ! " I said to myself. And at that moment, much as I detested him, Mr. Charles Ammidown appeared a happy angel in comparison with the murderous little fiend palpitating and shivering in my bed.

I thought of rushing to the head of the stairs and calling out, "Mr. Ammidown! don't trust yourself in that buggy."

He would ask, "Why not?" And I would say, "Some bad boys have been playing you a trick; they told me not to tell, but I — I " —

I was rehearsing my miserable part, when I heard his receding footsteps, followed by my sister's sweetly cordial " Good-night."

" Can you see?" she asked. And I knew she was standing there still, holding a light for him, while he unhitched his horse.

"Oh yes, very well, thank you," he replied from the street. " I am all right."

"*All right!* " thought I, in my lair.

There was a repetition of good-nights; the door closed; and I heard a sound of hoofs and buggy-wheels starting off confidently on the road.

Almost immediately, however, to my intent ears there came a noise of something like a crash; then an outcry; then a wilder sound of clattering hoofs and a rattling buggy.

The catastrophe had happened; and after the smash-up the horse was running away with the wrecked wagon.

Then came another cry, rather faint, but I was relieved to hear it, for it assured me that Ammidown was not killed outright.

But he was evidently hurt, and I felt that I ought to go at once to his assistance. Only my fears of exposure restrained me. I was supposed to be asleep in my bed ; and how could I, without betraying a previous knowledge of the trick played upon him, rush out, attracted by the sounds which even my sister, wide-awake down-stairs, did not hear ?

Silence followed that second faint cry; a terrible silence to me, lying there in an agony of anxiety and remorse, waiting to know the worst, and fearing I might be a murderer, after all. I pictured to myself Ammidown lying on the roadside after a few gasps, when a little timely aid might perhaps save his life.

Meanwhile I could hear my sister setting back chairs, shutting doors, and making other preparations for retiring.

Could I let her lock up the house and go to bed ignorant of the dreadful fact that the man who had just left her had been thrown from his buggy within twenty rods of her door, and was probably lying out there now with mangled flesh and broken limbs ?

I could endure the horrors of conscience no longer ; I resolved to start out of the house and find what had become of Ammidown, regardless of consequences. I had got my clothes half on, when there came a sound which struck terror to my soul, — a clumsy sort of thump on the front door.

Sister Marsh hastened to the entry, but seemed afraid at first to turn the key at such a summons.

" Who is there ? " she asked, standing, lamp in

hand; I listening, like the criminal I was, at the head of the stairs.

A faint voice outside answered. Then the door was opened. Then my sister exclaimed, in tones of amazement and consternation, —

"Mr. Ammidown! For mercy's sake! what has happened?"

"Don't be frightened," he replied, in a low voice. "I've had an overturn. I believe my shoulder is broken. Let me sit down here. I am very faint."

I had hardly had time to glide back to my room, when Sister Marsh sent a piercing scream for me up the attic stairs.

"Herbert! Come quick!" she called. "Mr. Ammidown has been thrown from his buggy and nigh-about killed. Do you hear?"

"What is the matter? Who is hurt?" I cried, running to the stairs, putting on my clothes, and pretending I had just been wakened from the sleep of the innocent.

Ammidown had sunk down on the threshold, like a drunken or dying man. He had lost his hat, his hair was tumbled over his eyes, his face and shirt-bosom were covered with dust and blood. Sister Marsh had set the lamp on the stairs, and was trying to keep him from tumbling over on the floor.

"How did it happen?" I said.

"Nobody knows. Oh, it is terrible! Run for the doctor as soon as you can!" my sister exclaimed. "Help me get him to the sofa first."

I took hold of the hurt shoulder, at which Ammidown gave a cry of pain and revived a little.

"A drop of — something!" he gasped.

"Wine!" said Sister Marsh. "Why didn't I think of it before?" And leaving me to support Ammidown, she flew to the cupboard.

He was soon able to get upon his feet with our assistance, and we helped him to the sofa. There I was glad enough to leave him in my sister's care and start for the doctor.

I ran out into the darkness, but had gone but a little way down the road when I heard somebody call my name, and stopped.

It was Josh Woods, who had remained hidden behind the fence with our two accomplices, "to see the fun," as he said.

"The buggy is all ripped to pieces! Is he hurt much?" he asked.

"Yes, almost killed," I answered. "What ever put it into your heads to do such a thing as that?"

"*You* put it into my head! You know you did!" he replied, resenting my implied reproach. "Now don't be so mean as to lay it all to us. Remember, we had nothing to do with it and know nothing about it. Come, boys!"

They were off and I was left alone. I ran all the way to the village, accompanied by a terrible shadow which I could not escape; the phantom of my own remorse and guilt.

As I approached the hotel, I met the landlord with

a lantern, just starting out to look for the missing man and the fragments of the vehicle. The horse had come home with a piece of it, and I could see more men, with another lantern, looking him carefully over as he stood panting and trembling under a shed.

The landlord got as much news out of me as I thought safe to tell, and appeared far more concerned for the broken buggy than for the injured driver.

"How do you suppose it happened?" I inquired, with as candid an air as I could assume.

"I don't know," he said. "Only I'm sure 'twan't my fault, nor the horse-and-buggy's. It will be a sorry job for somebody to pay for, I can tell ye!"

He appeared to aim this ominous remark at my own wretched little personality; and I can't say I found much comfort in it, as I hurried on to fetch the doctor.

CHAPTER III

HOW IT WORKED

Mr. Ammidown's injuries turned out to be bad enough, though fortunately not fatal.

"Oh yes, he'll get well," I heard the doctor say to Sister Marsh. "But it will hardly be safe to move him for a few days."

"There's no need of that," she replied. "As it was on my account that he received his hurts, I shall consider it a duty, as well as a privilege, to keep him here and take care of him."

There was nothing very pleasant for me to reflect upon in that. Whether she meant that Ammidown met with his accident in consequence of taking her to ride, or through the malice of some misguided friend or relative of her own, I was unable to decide. But one thing was clear; I hadn't succeeded very well in getting rid of the objectionable visitor. On the contrary, I had made him a permanent inmate of the house.

So much for my intermeddling. I could not have managed better, if I had tried, to bring him and my sister closer together, and give him opportunities for practising, not only on her vanity and credulity, but also on her womanly sympathies.

Strangely enough, I was not suspected of having a hand in causing the smash-up. Oh dear no! Marsh would never have believed her brother guilty of such conduct as that.

But when it was shown that it had been occasioned by the running off of a fore-wheel, — which had undoubtedly been tampered with, under cover of the darkness, while the buggy was standing at the gate, — she tightened her lips and said, with flushed cheeks and sparkling eyes, —

" I thought as much ! And I know who did it ! I know ! "

I did not dare to ask who. But Ammidown asked, from the sofa where he was lying, and brought out a significant reply.

" I'm not going to call names. But it's somebody that lives not far from here. Somebody who absurdly fancies he has a spite against you, Charles."

Mr. Ammidown was *Charles* to her — sometimes even *dear Charles* — ever since his catastrophe. He looked at her inquiringly ; he could not imagine whom she meant. But I could. In her heart she accused her rejected lover — our honest neighbor, Mr. Cole — of taking this revenge on his more favored rival !

That gave me almost as great a shock as if she had turned suddenly and denounced *me*. Mr. Cole and I were the best of friends, and I was indebted to him for many favors, — rides in his farm-wagon, maple sirup from his kettles in early spring, roasting-ears

from his corn-field, jokes and stories and pleasant
words whenever we chanced to meet.

How much of all this I owed to his partiality for
her I never stopped to inquire, but gave the credit of
it solely to his generous friendship and my own
attractive qualities. How could he help liking a fine
young fellow like me?

He had been deeply hurt by her rejection of him;
for the plain farmer had a sensitive nature under his
rough coat, and could feel as keenly as anybody a
wound to his love and pride. But I knew, if she did
not, how incapable he was of taking any such das-
tardly revenge.

I at first hoped that her words had been spoken in
haste, prompted by resentment of the bad opinion he
had expressed to me of her new suitor. But I soon
discovered, from some bitter things she flung out,
that she was firm in her conviction that Cole was the
culprit.

He had sent over to our house once or twice to
offer his neighborly services, and his messenger had
received curt replies. At last he came himself.

I met him at the door, and was trying hard to get
rid of him and prevent a scene, when Sister Marsh
appeared.

"I don't wish to be intrusive," he began, astonished and embarrassed by the look she gave him, for
though she had refused to marry him, her conduct
towards him hitherto had been at least kind and re-
spectful; "but I thought — under the circumstances
— I might perhaps be of some assistance."

"Thank you very much!" she replied, with biting sarcasm. "But we don't need any of the kind of assistance you would be likely to give. We have had too much of it already."

And tossing her head, my lady swept back scornfully into the house. Cole was left standing on the doorstep, a picture of amazement and distress. He turned appealingly to me.

"What have I done to offend her?" he asked.

I was as much troubled as he was, though in a very different way. Perhaps you think a boy who could do what I had done might afterwards stand coolly by and see an innocent man made to suffer for his fault. But I wasn't quite so bad as that.

"Don't mind now," I said in a low voice, walking away with him. "I told her what you said once of Ammidown; I am sorry now, for it did no good; it only made her mad."

"I am sorry too," he replied. "But you meant it for the best."

His kindness was coals of fire to me; and it was with a burning heart that I left him and went back into the house. I felt that I should be a great deal happier if I only had the courage to avow my own guilt and exonerate him; and I had half resolved to do so, even with the dreadful certainty before me that my sister would turn me out of doors in her wrath, and set me adrift on the world.

It was in vacation-time, and I had not much else to do but to wait upon her and her Charles. This I did with a humble submissiveness which might alone have been sufficient to excite suspicion. I was not habitually so meek. I actually became assistant nurse to the man I abhorred!

"As soon as he is gone," I said to myself, "I will tell my sister the truth, and take the consequences."

But though his recovery was rapid, and he might have returned to his hotel in a week, he found himself so comfortably provided for where he was, that I soon began to think he would never leave us at all.

In that, however, I was mistaken. He must make a trip to the city, he said, to transact some business. Then he must run home, but he would be back in ten days; a prospect which was far more cheering to my infatuated sister, you may be sure, than to me.

"If our railroad was completed," he remarked, in his large way, "I could step out and take a train at the new depot, which I trust we shall see built before another year. As it is, I shall take the stage-coach as it passes the door. No need of my going over to the village at all, if I can get some body to do an errand or two for me."

CHAPTER IV

HER BANK—BOOK

OF course, I was the boy to do his errands. And in five minutes I was on my way to the village with a written order, which I was to hand to his landlord.

I obeyed my instructions, and had the pleasure of seeing the hotel-keeper fly into a passion.

"Tell Ammidown," he cried, "that I sha'n't do anything of the kind. He must come and pay his bill. Is he afraid to show his face? You've carried off too many of his things already; I was foolish enough to let them go when he was sick. And now he wants me to put his trunk on the stage in the morning. Fancy!"

This outburst took place on the hotel steps; and it led to a discussion of Ammidown's character among the bystanders, which I was sorry my sister couldn't have heard. He had been so fully exposed as an impostor and swindler, that she alone appeared to cherish any confidence in him.

On my return I told him what the landlord had said, and that brought down upon me, from Sister Marsh, such a storm of reproaches for my frankness, that I found I had better keep to myself the other damaging things I had heard of him.

"He'll be gone to-morrow," I consoled myself by reflecting, "and then maybe she will come to her senses."

But that evening I overheard a conversation between them which filled me with fresh alarm. He had all along been talking to her persuasively of investing her money in the stock of the new railroad company; and I now discovered that she had made up her mind to take his disinterested advice.

After going up-stairs, with the intention of going to bed, I had come down again for some matches, when I was stopped in the entry by what I heard and saw through the partly open door.

My sister had her bank-book on her knee and a pen in her hand, as if about to write something, while he sat beside her, arguing in an earnest voice. His back was towards me; but a lamp on the table shone full on the open bank-book, the hand that held the pen, and her flushed face as she listened.

"It's as plain as day and as certain as anything can be in this world," he was saying. "You get only about sixty dollars a year on your twelve hundred now. But I can invest it so that you will get five or six times that."

And he went on to repeat what he had often said of his influence with the company, which he proposed now to make use of in obtaining stock for her at "bottom prices: just what I and the directors themselves have to pay," he explained.

"Well, of course, I shall be guided by you," she

said, and signed her name to something which appeared to have been already written on a blank page of the bank-book.

He commended her good sense, as he was fond of doing, looked at the writing and nodded with satisfaction.

"Your interest is mine, Marcia," says he; "and as I am a man of honor and your best friend, you will find you've made a magnificent investment."

With which rather doubtful assurance he took possession of the book, placing it carefully in his breast-pocket.

"There goes her twelve hundred dollars!" I said to myself, with suppressed fury, hardly able to keep from rushing in, denouncing his villany and snatching away the book.

But what good would that do?

None whatever. So I restrained myself, and crept back silently up the dark staircase without the matches, the search for which had led me to make this exasperating discovery.

The stage-coach took him up the next morning, when there was something in his look at parting from us which I am sure must have given her a glimpse into his true character. After so long playing a difficult and irksome game, relief and triumph at last! That's what it said. As if, at the final moment, his mask had fallen off.

Yes, that look had gone to Sister Marsh's heart. She became absent-minded, full of anxious thoughts and fitful sighs ; going to the door every ten minutes and looking up and down, and then returning to her work, which she would hold in her lap without taking a stitch.

I could see that her suspicions of Mr. Charles were fully roused, now that he had got her bank-book and gone out of her sight.

"Is anything the matter, Marsh?" I asked, hoping to get her confidence.

" No — nothing — only " — she was up again and at the door — " I was wondering how long it would take for you to get a horse and drive me to the city."

" To the city ! " I said, knowing very well she was thinking of the bank-book. " Why didn't you go in the stage with Mr. Ammidown ? "

" I wish I had ! " she exclaimed. " But I didn't think of it. Something has occurred to me since."

" It will take a good while if I go to the village for a horse," I said. " But if I could borrow one of Mr. Cole's " —

She interrupted me. " I wouldn't send to him for a horse, if I never had one, and if I never went to the city ! Never mind. It's a foolish notion I've got — very foolish ! " And she returned to her work.

"Sister Marsh," I said, "if it has anything to do with Mr. Ammidown — any misgiving about him — it isn't foolish at all. You'd better let me get a horse somewhere as soon as I can, and follow the scamp."

That was the most injudicious thing I could have
said. She was changed in a twinkling. Suspicion
of her Charles turned at once to anger against me;
and in championing him she forgot her fears.

"He is the most disinterested, the most honorable
man I ever saw!" she exclaimed, at the end of a
violent tirade against me and Neighbor Cole and all
the rest of Ammidown's enemies. "If I have dis-
trusted him for a moment, I am ashamed of myself."

"Shall I go for a horse?" I asked. "You might
yet be in time."

"Of course not!" she replied emphatically. "I
didn't know what I was saying. My trust in him is
boundless!"

Nevertheless, I could see that she was not happy;
and I have no doubt but that she wished more than
once during the afternoon that she had let me fetch
a horse.

Her distrust having been once awakened, there
was only one man who could reason her out of it,
and that was Ammidown himself. I wanted to tell
her now all about the cause of his accident; but in
her irritated state I didn't dare mention his name.

She expected a letter from him the next day. It
did not come. She was greatly disturbed. And
when I returned a second and a third time from the
post-office without a word from her Charles, she no
longer attempted to conceal her distress.

Then an engineer, who was assisting to make
some changes in the line of the projected rail-

road, came to the door one afternoon for a glass of water.

"I suppose," said Sister Marsh as she gave it to him, "that the depot out here behind my orchard is a settled thing."

He looked up over the glass in some surprise and answered, —

"I have never heard of any depot this side of the village. Have you?"

"Why, yes, certainly! Mr. Ammidown told me" — Sister Marsh began, and hesitated, quite overcome by the look of amused scorn that came into the man's eyes.

"Ammidown! that fellow!" he laughed. "I wonder if he has been humbugging you too?"

"What do you mean?" says Sister Marsh, in a flutter of excitement. "Don't your directors know him?"

"They know him to their sorrow," he replied, "as a confounded bore and impostor."

"Has he no influence with them — no interest in the" — She could not finish the sentence.

"In the road? No interest, and no influence whatever. His game is to get people to think he has, and borrow money on the strength of favors he promises them. I trust," said the engineer, after taking a sip of water, "that he hasn't borrowed any money of you?"

"No," she said, and her agitation was truly pitiful to witness. "But I've given him all I have to invest

for me in the company's stock. That is good,
isn't it?"

"It is good," he replied, "if you can get it. But
if you have trusted him to buy it for you, I'm afraid
you will never see your stock nor your money again."

"I can't believe it of him!" gasped my sister,
leaning against the door-post, and looking deathly
sick.

"Well, believe in him as long as you can, if it's
too late to get your money back," he said, starting
to hand her the glass, but changing his mind and
handing it to me.

"I fear it is too late," she managed to reply, with
her white, trembling lips. "I gave him my bank-
book, with an order, filled out and signed, for the
money. I was to have heard from him before this."

"I am afraid you never will hear from him," the
man answered kindly. "I am very sorry for you,
madam." And with these terrible words he went
away.

For terrible they were to Sister Marsh. She drew
back into the house, sank upon the first chair, and
gave way to hysterical tears.

CHAPTER V

WHO PAID FOR THE BROKEN BUGGY

I WAS glad to see she thought so much of the loss of her money; for that showed she might yet be consoled for the loss of her lover.

"Now is my time to tell her," I said to myself. And I was considering how I should begin a revelation I had to make, when the engineer returned.

"It is not pleasant to be the bearer of bad news," he said, looking in at the door. "But my companion out here tells me something which I think you ought to know. He says Ammidown was arrested yesterday, for getting money under false pretences."

"Arrested?" said my sister.

"Yes; he saw it in a morning paper. There were officers after him, when he left the city; but he had got as far as Albany before he was caught."

"I wish they had caught him before!" said Sister Marsh. Then, turning to me, "Get a horse as soon as you can! I know it is too late; he is gone with my money; but I'll hurry to town and see about it, as I ought to have done before — and would have done, if I hadn't been a fool!"

"Where shall I get a horse?" I asked.

"Anywhere!" she exclaimed. "Get Mr. Cole's, if he will let us have it, after such treatment as he has received from me. I don't approve of what he did; but he meant it for my good, and it would have been well, perhaps, if that man had been killed."

"Sister Marsh," said I, almost as excited as she was, "I'll get the horse, but I want to tell you something first. Will you come here?"

Wondering what I had to reveal, she followed me to her own room, where I opened a bureau-drawer and took from under some clothing in a corner of it a piece of paper.

"Read that," I said, putting it into her hands.

It was the order-page of her bank-book, with the form of an order on the Treasurer of the City Five Cent Savings-Bank, filled out and signed by her own hand : —

"Pay to Mr. Charles Ammidown, or Bearer, any part or the whole of my deposit No. 1927.
MARCIA BLAINE."

"Herbert!" she exclaimed in the greatest astonishment. "Where did you get this?"

"I have done one foolish thing," I replied; "and I hope this won't turn out to be another."

"Foolish!" she cried, wild with joy. "Why, it's my order for the money! How could he draw the deposit without it? He couldn't!"

"So I thought," I explained. "And I was so

sure he was going to rob you, that I took the bank-book from his pocket that morning when he was blacking his boots — he had left his coat hanging over a chair in his room — and tore out the order. I wanted to keep the book itself, but was afraid he would miss it before he got away. So I put that back, and kept this."

"Bless you for a prudent, noble, darling brother!" she exclaimed, hugging me in her ecstasy. "You've saved me from the poor-house in my old age. But get the horse all the same. I must go to the bank as soon as hoofs and wheels can carry me."

Cole was glad to let us have the horse. On the way to the city — a drive of nine miles — I made a full confession to her of my other secret.

"Well, Herbert, I declare!" she said, "I never believed you would do so wicked a thing as that. But of course I forgive you. It might have been worse. And I am rejoiced to know Mr. Cole had nothing to do with it. I certainly owe him very ample amends for the wrong I have done him."

We found her deposit safe in the bank; and I for one had a good laugh over the treasurer's description of Ammidown coming in that forenoon after he left us, producing the bank-book at the counter, opening it with a cheerful confidence which changed to surprise as he turned the leaves, and finally grew to wrath and chagrin when he found the order-page had been torn out.

Luckily the pursuit of the officers who were on

his track gave him no time to return to my sister
for an explanation; and he had gone off, of course,
without the money.

As for the lost bank-book, the treasurer said it
would make no difference to the owner whether it
was recovered or not; he would, if necessary, give
her a new one.

The excitement of the chase over, Sister Marsh
was thoughtful, but not so very unhappy, on the way
home.   At length she said, —

"I don't think we owe that man anything for the
accident you caused him.   But he never paid for
the broken buggy."

"I mean to do that," I said, "with the first money
I can earn."

"I am glad to hear you say so," she replied.
"Meanwhile, we will stop at the blacksmith's and
tell him to send the bill to me.   I think I can well
afford to settle it, after what you have saved me.
Then there is poor Mr. Cole! what reparation *can* I
make to him?"

I was relieved to find that the mending of the
buggy was to cost only about twelve dollars.

Another thing, which happened three months
later, rejoiced me still more.   The reparation she
made "poor Mr. Cole," was to encourage a renewal
of his visits, and to give an answer which pleased
him particularly well, the next time he asked her to
marry him.

"HE FOUND THE ORDER-PAGE HAD BEEN TORN OUT." — Page 127.

UNCLE CALEB'S ROAN COLT

CHAPTER I

"I WANT TO BORROW SOME MONEY"

Mr. Caleb Crowfoot, old bachelor and farmer,
was standing in his stable door one September
morning, regarding his poultry and calves with satisfaction, when a ruddy-featured youth of seventeen
opened the sagging and creaking gate far enough to
allow his rather sturdy body to squeeze through, and
entered the yard.

"Good-morning, Uncle Caleb!" he said, with a
cheerful air, unterrified by the big cock-turkey that
puffed and strutted and drummed and gobbled at
him.

"Good-morning! good-morning, Hartley!" Uncle
Caleb replied, scratching his jaw, with a curious,
good-natured grin, while he said to himself, "Wonder what he has come for, this time o' day! How
are all the folks?" he added, aloud.

"Fair to middling," Hartley Hollsworth answered,
a certain native frankness of manner fast getting the

better of some evident embarrassment he felt in con-
fronting Mr. Crowfoot. "Uncle, I've come to you
on what you may think a foolish sort of business."

"Very likely!" laughed the farmer. "What is
it?"

"I want to borrow some money."

Uncle Caleb's grin became a trifle ghastly.

"What do you want of money?" he asked.

"Well, you see, uncle, there are a good many of us
there at home; more than the old farm can provide
for, as we grow up. And I've a notion of striking
out for myself," Hartley explained.

"Which way do you propose to strike?" Uncle
Caleb inquired.

"I want to fit myself for some kind of business,"
said the boy, "and I've made up my mind that if I
could go to a good commercial school for a few
months, I could save a great deal of time, and fit myself for a better situation than I might perhaps work
up to in as many years, with just the common school
education I have."

Seeing that Uncle Caleb was not quite thunder-
struck by the proposal, Hartley had courage to continue:—

"Mind, I don't want to beg a cent of you or anybody; but I thought perhaps you might be willing to
trust me with a little, which I am sure will be more
help to me now than thousands might be by and by.
I'll pay you interest, and I'll repay the principal of
the loan as sure as I live. You know I'm no trifler;

you know that what I say I mean, and that's why I come to you, Uncle Caleb."

There was something exceedingly honest, earnest, and engaging in the boy's face as he spoke. Uncle Caleb's smile flickered, and he scratched his jaw once more.

"Why don't you go to your father? He's the man to help you, if anybody."

"He might help me, perhaps, if he chose. I don't know. He has had a pretty hard time to worry along with his large family, and now he thinks, as we get old enough to work, we ought to stay at home and help him."

"Don't you think so yourself, Hartley?"

"I think we ought to do all we can to help him, and to help each other; but I am convinced I can do more for myself and all concerned by striking out. He is willing, but he won't give me a cent to start with. Mother believes more in my plans than he does, and she advised me to apply to you."

"She was always a good sister to me, and she's a good mother to you, Hartley," was the old bachelor's reflection, as he gave his jaw another scraping.

"The best of mothers!" was the boy's fervent response.

"How much money do you want?" Uncle Caleb asked.

"I hardly know; in the neighborhood of a hundred dollars; I shall try to make that do."

Mr. Crowfoot coughed, and his countenance settled into a dubious expression.

"I haven't got any money; I haven't got a hundred dollars. If I had, I don't know — I might let you have it. H'm!" and he mused.

"If I could have a little at a time; if I could have the promise of it all in the course of the fall and winter," Hartley began to explain.

"I can't make any promises for the futur'," said the old bachelor. "Sorry, my boy, but" —

Hartley was turning away disheartened, with a murmured excuse for having troubled his uncle, who called after him.

"I haven't a dollar of money to spare; but I'll tell you, Hartley; there's that roan colt. If he'll be of any service to you, you can take him."

Alternate hope and humorous despair crossed the ruddy, youthful features.

"It's a fine colt, uncle," he said, as he eyed the long-tailed, rough-coated young horse frisking at the flies in the shadow of the shed.

"Fine! I tell ye!" exclaimed Uncle Caleb. "Four years old last spring; well broke to pull in harness, single or double; sound in wind and limb; nary blemish about him."

"Very fine!" responded Hartley. "But what can I do with him? I can't ride him to and from school, and if I could, his keep would cost me more than my railroad fares. Will you sell him?"

"No, no, I won't sell that colt! He's too valoo'ble an animal for the price he would bring this time o' year; but you may take him and do the best you can with him ; get as much edecation out of him as a fine, four-year-old roan colt will bring."

"May I pledge him as security in borrowing the money ? " Hartley eagerly inquired.

"Yes, I don't know but you may, with some good man that will keep him along, and not work him too hard," said Uncle Caleb. "You ought to raise a hundred and twenty-five dollars on him, and let him work out the interest. I calculate that colt will be worth more a year from now than he is now, if he ain't overworked ; so I guess I can afford it, if you can find the right kind of a man."

"What if the colt should die ? " Hartley asked.

"If he dies from any ordinary disease, I'll stand the loss ; but if from any accident, or neglect, or anything the man is responsible for, the loss shall be his'n. That's fair, ain't it ? "

Hartley thought it was fair, and said he would come back for the colt as soon as he could find a market for him.

"No, no, take him now ! " cried Uncle Caleb. "You must have the colt to show when you go to make the bargain ; and you'll want him to ride to find your man. You must let me know who 'tis that wants him, and just what he agrees to, before you clinch the trade."

Hartley thought it an exceedingly odd arrange- ment ; but he accepted it joyfully, and talked it over with Uncle Caleb as they bridled the colt, and gave his rough coat a good rubbing-down.

"Now, my boy," said Mr. Crowfoot, as Hartley mounted Roan's bare back, "ride over to Dr. Waring's the first thing. He has been at me to get this colt. He wants a second horse, and there's no danger of his driving one too hard. If he'll take him on your terms, then I'll see about having the agreement put in writing."

"He can keep him one year?" cried Hartley.

"One year, or till you pay back the money," replied Uncle Caleb. "I know the doctor pretty well; and, to tell the truth, he is about the only man I am willing to let have the colt. You must insist on a hundred and twenty-five, for that's what he offered me for him a month ago, and the dicker may turn out to be a sale, you know."

"You think I may never redeem him?" said Hartley. "You'll see if I don't, uncle, if I live and have my health."

And the boy rode off, high in hope, to offer Roan to Dr. Waring. Uncle Caleb gazed after him from the gate with a benevolent smile, and scratched his jaw.

"I always meant to do something for the boys," he said, "and I'm glad to do it in this way. 'Tain't like taking so much money out o' my own pocket," which was always a distressing operation to old bachelor Caleb; he himself confessed that he "hated it wus'n pizen."

CHAPTER II

"MY VERY FIRST EARNINGS"

HARTLEY had a gleeful ride to the doctor's house, about two miles distant, and the good luck to find him at home. The doctor listened to his proposal with a droll smile, and asked why Crowfoot didn't sell the colt outright.

"I don't know; uncle is queer about some things," replied Hartley. "If you should pay him the money, he couldn't bear to let it go out of his hands again; but he is willing to lend the colt."

"Well! well!" exclaimed the doctor, looking the animal carefully over. "I'm glad to take him, for your sake as well as for the sake of the colt. I'll drive him over to your uncle's this afternoon, and fix the thing in writing."

Uncle Caleb did not see much more of his hopeful nephew for over a year. He knew that the boy was studying hard, and afterward heard that he had at length left the commercial school to accept a salaried situation.

It was on Thanksgiving Day of the following year that Hartley again called on his uncle. His cheeks were not quite so ruddy as when we first made his acquaintance, but he was perceptibly taller and more manly in his bearing.

In response to Mr. Crowfoot's inquiries as to his progress and prospects, he said, putting out his cane at the same old turkey-cock, who came at him with bristling plumage and wattles flashing from purple to scarlet : —

"I certainly hoped to bring back that colt to-day, uncle, but " —

"You're disapp'inted!" laughed the old bachelor. "Well, to tell the truth, Hartley, *I* should have been disapp'inted if you'd brought him. I never expected you would. You've done your best, I've no doubt. I hear you've been industrious, and finally got a good place, and that's enough for me. I'm in no hurry to get the colt back."

"I'm glad to hear you say that," Hartley replied. "For when I went to the doctor's for him just now, he said he couldn't spare him, and he didn't believe you would have any use for him before next spring. He has quite fallen in love with Roan, uncle."

"Ah, I knew he would!" and Mr. Crowfoot scratched his jaw with satisfaction.

"So now," continued the youth, "I want to know what I shall do with the money?"

"What money?" Uncle Caleb stopped scratching his jaw and stared.

"Why, the money for the colt!" said Hartley, taking a roll of bills from his pocket. "If you are willing the doctor should keep him till spring, I may as well pay it to you."

"Money for the colt!" repeated Crowfoot, astonished. "How did you come by it?"

"I earned it!" replied Hartley proudly. "It's my very first earnings, — except a little of it, which I managed to save out of the doctor's loan, living at home as I have done most of the time, and doing some work to pay for my board. The loan has been of the greatest service to me, uncle, and I can't tell you how much obliged I am to you for it."

"But I — I don't want to take your money, Hartley," said the old bachelor. "Don't you need it — a little longer?"

"If you don't particularly wish it," Hartley answered, "I have a use for it in view. Sister Annie, you know, is a very good pianist, considering the limited advantages she has had. She is beginning to earn a little money by giving lessons.

"But she finds she could get a much better class of pupils, and earn a great deal more money, if she could learn the new method of fingering taught now by the best teachers. I mean that she shall take lessons of Professor Wasbach as soon as I have money to pay for them ; and if I can have *this* money for the purpose — why, uncle, it will be an unexpected good fortune!"

"Of course! of course!" cried Uncle Caleb gleefully. "Let the roan colt dance to the music!"

Much as he loved money in his purse, this money out of it was beginning to give him more satisfaction than all his hoarded gains.

"I tell you what, boy!" he chuckled; "that roan colt is a pooty good hoss, ain't he, now?"

"He's pulling us through!" laughed the grateful nephew; and he went off to carry the good news to the doctor, and to his elder sister Annie.

Uncle Caleb should have witnessed the girl's de- lighted surprise when told that, through his liberality, she would be enabled to commence taking lessons of the celebrated professor at once. The very next day she went to the city with Hartley, saw the great Wasbach, played to him, won his approval, and made arrangements to come to him for two lessons a week during the winter.

Meanwhile, wholly unconscious of the good he was doing, the roan colt jogged about town with the doc- tor on his morning rounds, and munched his hay and oats with the peace of mind of a well-fed horse doing his daily duties, which a kind master made easy to him.

CHAPTER III

"MORE OF THAT COLT MONEY"

UNCLE CALEB was a little grayer, and nephew Hartley was a trifle more stocky, and both were a year older, when they met one afternoon at the village post-office.

"How happens it you are not at your place of business?" asked the old bachelor.

"I got off this afternoon, as I have an errand at the savings-bank; and, to tell the truth," Hartley added, "I was going over to call on you."

"Always glad to see you," said Uncle Caleb, holding the young man's hand with the interest we feel in those we are trying to benefit. "Anything special?"

"Well, yes," replied Hartley, with a smile quivering around the corners of his mouth. "Annie and I have got some money deposited for you in the savings-bank."

"Money for me!" exclaimed the old bachelor, affecting surprise, and trying to frown, while his heart-strings were tickling with the keenest pleasure.

"Yes; more of that colt money," said Hartley. "Her lessons in town have been expensive, but she has been earning more and more, while she has been making wonderful improvement under Wasbach's instruction. We've helped the folks at home a good deal, and now we've got a hundred and twenty-five dollars in the bank, with some interest. And I want to know what I'm to do with it."

Uncle Caleb looked contemplative, rasping his jaw.

" Does the doctor want to git rid o' the roan colt ? " he asked.

" I rather think not ! " said Hartley.

" Well, I don't need the hoss," mused Uncle Caleb. " And, fact is, I'd rather he should be doing good in his humble way. You rode him a year, as 'twere. And now Annie has been on his back a year longer, so to speak. Ain't there nobody else in the family that wants to be carried over a rough place ? "

" Uncle ! you're the kindest uncle in the world ! " Hartley exclaimed, in a voice choked with emotion. " I thought I'd see what you would say before I mentioned it ; but there is my brother Roland. He's a natural student, and he has made up his mind he must go to college."

" Business college? " said Uncle Caleb.

" No ; he wants a regular course of study at one of the great universities. And Annie and I think it would be a good thing. Thanks to you for helping us, we shall be in a position to help him. He can help himself, too, by teaching a little, if necessary. Mother approves the plan, and father don't say much against it, since he will not be called on for money. In fact, he is beginning to believe a little more in us children than he did."

"And you'd like to put Roland on the roan colt — let him take his turn a-ridin' him?" laughed the uncle.

"It would be a very great help to him!" exclaimed Hartley. "If he could have the use of the money — or the colt — for a year or two "—

"Or three or four years!" struck in the merry old bachelor, rubbing his jaw vivaciously. "Boy, I never had such a colt! He beats all the hosses I ever owned, or expect to own! Now let him gallop with Roland through college!"

Time galloped with the colt, and it seemed to Uncle Caleb hardly two years, instead of five, when he received an invitation to attend the graduating exercises of Roland's class. He could not believe at first that the boy was really through college; and then he declared that he couldn't think of such a thing as accepting the invitation. He had no "clo'es to wear," for one thing.

But Annie ironed a shirt for him, and Hartley persuaded him that he needed a new plain suit for Sunday, adding, "If you feel you can't afford it, uncle, why, there's a little of that colt money in the bank, I believe."

Mr. Crowfoot concluded he could afford almost anything for such an occasion; he accompanied the family, and sat through the exercises and listened, proud and happy, to Roland's Latin oration, without understanding a word of it, of course, but applauding it nevertheless with all the might of his big farmer's hands.

When all was over, he averred that "he hadn't enjoyed a circus so, he didn't know when;" it being a performance in which he saw only one horse, and that a certain roan colt.

But the colt was a sedate, middle-aged horse by this time, and the question soon came up, who was to ride him next?

Barker, the fourth boy, liked the farm, and early decided to stay at home and work with his father. Winchell, the third son, had already gone into a newspaper and job-printing office in the village, and was doing well, when he had an opportunity to buy out one of the proprietors.

Hartley was cashier in a large importing house in the city; Annie was teaching music, and Roland, immediately after graduating, turned to teaching school; they could all help Winchell a little in the purchase, which, however, would require all the money they could raise, and a little more.

"Put in the roan colt!" cried Uncle Caleb, when he heard how the matter stood. "He's been through college, and now we'll see how he'll do in a printin'-office." It would have done you good to see him laugh, rub his jaw, and "vow" that he had never seen "such lots o' fun got out of a hoss in all his born days!"

CHAPTER IV

A WEDDING PRESENT

THE colt did very well indeed in the newspaper and job business ; and the very first debt which Winchell paid off was the one which the whole family felt to be somehow sacred, — the one owing for Uncle Caleb's roan.

Since Roland's graduation, the old bachelor had formed a habit of going more into society than he had been accustomed to do before ; and on a certain Thanksgiving Day he drove over to dine with his relatives, the Hollsworths.

He was one of the jolliest of a rather jolly family group. Hartley was there, and Annie, and Roland the school-teacher, and Winchell the printer and editor, and Barker the farmer, and Henrietta the second daughter, and Julia the youngest ; with the proud and affectionate mother, and the father, who had learned by this time that such active, helpful and self-helping children could not always be kept, like babes, under parental control, and that, even if they could be, it would not be well for him or them to keep them so.

In the glow of friendly feeling which suffused all

hearts during the great Thanksgiving dinner, Hartley made a little speech, in which he told, in his
quaintly humorous way, the story of the roan colt,
and at the close informed Uncle Caleb that the said
useful animal was once more in the stable, and
awaited his orders.

" In the stable ! what do you mean ? " cried the old
bachelor excitedly, staring over his poised knife and
fork.

" In other words," said Hartley, — a sturdy, whis-
kered Hartley now, — " the money is in the savings-
bank again, and now you must either take that or the
colt — if, indeed, Dr. Waring will consent to part
with his favorite."

" Look here !" said Uncle Caleb, dropping his
knife, in order to lift his hand and give his jaw
a rasping, " I never had so much good out of any
critter I ever owned, and I — I couldn't think of taking money for him myself. Don't some of the rest
of you want to go to college, or to buy out a business,
or something ? "

" I believe we are all provided for at present," said
Hartley. "Barker sticks to the farm, and Julia will
stay at home, for a while anyway. As for Henrietta
— may I tell ? Of course I can tell, Uncle Caleb
being one of the family ! "

Henrietta said : " Oh yes ; you may tell *him*,"
blushing charmingly.

" Well," said Hartley, " Henrietta is provided for,
too, in a way very satisfactory to all of us. She is

going to marry the young minister, — Roland's friend, you know, Mr. Galt."

"It was while I was riding the roan that I made his acquaintance, and brought him here to visit us," said Roland.

"Then we owe even Henrietta's husband to the colt!" exclaimed Uncle Caleb, shaking with sympathetic mirth. "I said before that he beat all the critters that ever set foot on my farm ; and now this caps the climax."

Hartley sent the pitcher of new cider around the table, and proposed the health of the roan colt. The toast was gleefully received, and Uncle Caleb responded : —

" It wouldn't be right for me to get any more good out of that roan than I've got already ; and he never shall be sold. What'll we do with him ? That's a question common-sense and gratitude can easily answer. The young parson will want a hoss in his family, and Henrietty shall have him for a weddin' present ! "

RODNEY HOBART'S MEMORY

CHAPTER I

"AN INTERESTING HEAD"

"WELL, good luck to you, Rodney! Keep a good heart. Something will turn up for a stout lad like you, I am sure."

Rodney Hobart, an orphan boy of sixteen, had gone out into the world to seek for employment, and stopped over night at Farmer Hamil's. It was the fall of the year, and the farmer had no work for him; but he had kind words and good wishes, and a hearty hand-shake for the homeless boy as they parted the next morning.

Rodney thanked him as well as he could; but his heart was too full to say much, and he was not a lad of many words at any time.

Farmer Hamil had taken a great liking to his quiet ways, dry humor, and shrewd sense; and now, seeing him turn away from the door with his little bundle under his arm, going to look for work and a home, he knew not where, the good man's heart yearned after him, and he called out again, —

"If you find you can't do any better, come back here, and I'll keep you over night again, or as long as you want to stay."

"Thank you," said Rodney, in a low voice, and with an odd twitching of the lips, which the farmer saw and understood. "But I think I can find something to do."

He wandered on, asking for work by the way, and in the course of the forenoon entered one of those new and thriving Western towns, which have grown from villages to cities within a very few years.

To a careless observer, Rodney's appearance was not prepossessing. His clothes were worn and patched, and his limbs had grown rather too long for his sleeves and trousers. He wore his hat on the back of his head, and he had that way of staring about him which is vulgarly termed "gawky." Carrying his bundle under his arm, and looking into all the shop windows, he excited more than one good-natured smile among those he passed or met, and was really as much an object for pleasant ridicule as young Ben Franklin eating his loaf of bread in the streets of Philadelphia a hundred and fifty years before.

He came at length to a window in which were some phrenological heads, and charts mapping out the different organs ; and noticing that the shop seemed to be open to the public, he walked into it.

Some of the shelves were occupied by books, while others held busts of remarkable characters, all of which Rodney viewed with a good deal of interest.

There were other spectators in the shop, one of whom, a well-dressed man in side-whiskers, Rodney looked at as sharply as he did at any of the busts, and then did not appear to notice him any more.

Seeing a gentleman come out once or twice from a sort of private office behind the shop, the lad made up his mind that he was one of the proprietors, and, watching for a good chance, finally stepped up and accosted him.

"Do you want to hire a boy?"

"Can't say that I do," the man replied, and was turning away hastily, when he stopped and looked more carefully at the verdant youth who stood before him, in short trousers, and with the hat on the back of his head. "No," he added, "I don't want to hire a boy; but one thing I should like, which perhaps will be a good thing for you."

"What's that?" said Rodney.

"I don't know whether you are aware of it, but you have a rather extraordinary head. I'd like to see your hat off and examine your head, if you've no objection."

Rodney answered in his silent way, by pulling off his hat and standing, with a humorous smile, for the phrenologist to proceed.

"An interesting head," said the phrenologist.

"It's an interesting head to me," said Rodney. "I should like to know what you make of it."

"Step into the office. Sit down. Walk in, gentlemen, and you may have an opportunity of seeing how much there is in our science."

The spectators entered the back room accordingly, and Rodney found himself the centre of an interested group.

"In the first place," said the phrenologist, laying his fingers on the boy's forehead, "you have wonderful perceptive faculties, and a wonderful memory. You see everything, and you remember everything. How is it, my boy?"

"I generally see what there is to be seen, and I don't remember that I ever forgot anything," said Rodney.

"If you ever had forgotten, you would remember it," said the phrenologist with a smile. "How long had you been in that room when you spoke to me?"

"About twenty minutes."

"And how much do you think you can tell me about it?"

"I can tell you what the busts are, and where they are."

"I've no doubt of it. Tell us what busts are on the first lower shelf by the door."

"The bust nearest the door," replied Rodney, looking straight down at his knees, "is Daniel Webster. The one next to it is a Caffre negro."

"Right," said the man with side-whiskers, looking back at the busts. "Anybody might have noticed and remembered those. See if he can tell us what is on the upper shelf, opposite the door."

"There's nothing on that shelf but a paper box and a few dusty pamphlets," said Rodney.

"Well, that's so; but it isn't much to remember," said the man. "Take the shelf below it. First — well, what is first?"

"First at the left," replied Rodney, "is Bryant, the poet — if you mean that. At the other end of the shelf is Black Hawk, the Indian chief."

"Right again! That's curious!" said the man. "Now the fourth bust from the right, on the same shelf?"

"John Hotton, the murderer," answered Rodney promptly.

"You're slightly wrong there," said the phrenologist. "The man's name is Holton, John Holton."

"The label says, 'John Hotton,' I'm pretty sure," said Rodney.

"Well, I declare," said one of the spectators, stepping up to the bust, "the boy is more right than wrong. The *l* is made very much like the *t*, and both letters are crossed."

After this it was found that Rodney could tell the names and places of all the organs on the phrenological charts, and also the titles of many of the books on the shelves. The spectators expressed great astonishment, while the phrenologist smiled with satisfaction.

"Can you remember faces and people as well as you can things of this sort?" asked the man with side-whiskers.

"I can, I think, remember any face I ever saw, or any name I ever heard, I don't care how many years ago," said Rodney quietly. "This is nothing new to me. What else is there in my head?"

"You think a great deal, and say very little. You have large conscientiousness and caution, and very large firmness, with but moderate self-esteem, which makes you slow and careful about making up your mind as to any course, while it is just about impossible to change you when you think you are right."

CHAPTER II

FARMER HAMIL'S HAY

RODNEY laughed. "I reckon there's something in phrenology," he said dryly. "But I should like to know what business I am best fitted for."

"You might succeed in almost anything. But you would be invaluable in any position where thorough integrity, and a quick perception and faultless memory of a great variety of details are required."

"He is just the person I want!" spoke up the well-dressed man with side-whiskers. "I run the Great Western Hotel; I have so many transient customers that it is sometimes the hardest thing in the world to keep track of them, and I often lose money in consequence. I want somebody to look after those who come and go, and don't pay, and I think this boy will fill the place better than anybody."

Strangely enough, Rodney did not look up or make any reply to this speech. The man added, —

"I'll give you twenty dollars a month, and your board and clothes, if you can do what I ask, and if you want to hire out."

Still Rodney looked down and said not a word. He was thinking.

"He asked me just now if I wanted to hire a boy," said the phrenologist. "What do you think?" turning to Rodney. "This man is Mr. Belmain ; he has one of the largest hotels in the State, and I should say it was just the place for you."

Rodney lifted his eyes, and gave one more look at the man he had scrutinized so sharply at first. Then he said dryly, and with evident reluctance, —

"I can't well refuse such an offer, and if I don't find something else to do before night I'll accept it."

"You won't hear of any such wages offered to a boy of your age, I'm very sure of that," said the hotel-keeper. "Engage yourself to me, and I'll take you right over to the clothing-store, put you into a new suit, and set you about your new business this very afternoon."

Rodney still hesitated, walked about the room, looked out of the window, pitched his hat on the back of his head again, and at last said gravely, "I'll go."

That very afternoon our hero, whom we first beheld a ragged and homeless wanderer going from Farmer Hamil's door, found himself in a new suit of clothes, and a situation which might have turned a foolish boy's head. But there was no vanity about Rodney. He devoted himself faithfully to his employer's interests, and not only "kept track" of transient customers, but did almost a man's work besides.

His good fortune did not cause Rodney to forget

the man who had been so kind to him; and knowing that Mr. Belmain wished to buy a quantity of hay for his stables, he said he knew a man who had some to sell. This gave him an opportunity to pay Farmer Hamil a visit.

The farmer was delighted to see his young friend again, and to hear of his good luck.

" Well, well, twenty dollars a month! And you like the place? Why, that's splendid! And how do you think the place likes you?"

"I don't know," replied Rodney. ". Mr. Belmain doesn't say a word about that, so I just go ahead and do my best. Only one thing troubles me a little, and I'd like to ask you a question."

"Well, ask away, only don't go to putting any of your old tough conundrums, you know."

"It's no conundrum. But I — I'll just suppose a case," said Rodney. "Suppose you knew a man who had committed some crime, and gone off to another country, and begun new, and seemed to be getting along pretty well, would you think it your duty to expose him?"

"Well, my lad," said Farmer Hamil, whittling a stick, "that's a tough one, after all! Seems to me, if he was a bad and dangerous man, I'd think I ought to expose him; but if he was trying to do better, I don't see how I could, any way in the world. I should want to give the poor fellow a chance."

· Rodney's face lightened. "I'm glad to hear you say that. I feel just so myself."

"Do you know such a man?"

"Please don't ask me any questions, Mr. Hamil. And now," said Rodney, quickly changing the subject, "let's talk about the hay."

Mr. Belmain had offered a good price for first-class redtop and timothy, and Mr. Hamil was glad to sell his crop to so good a customer. The next day, and the next, and the day after, loads of hay went from his stacks to the capacious lofts over the hotel stables. When all had been delivered, he came into the hotel, pulled off his hat, and took out of the crown a bill for one hundred and thirty dollars, which he handed to the landlord.

"All right," said Mr. Belmain cheerfully. "Call next week and I will settle with you."

CHAPTER III

"A MOLE ON YOUR RIGHT CHEEK, MR. BELMAIN"

RODNEY, who stood by and overheard the remark, gave Farmer Hamil an anxious look, and afterwards followed him to the door.

"Why didn't you urge the payment?" he said. "He has the money right there in the safe; he might have paid you."

"I know that," replied the farmer, "and that's what makes me feel so easy about it."

"Be sure and get your pay next time," whispered Rodney at parting.

When Mr. Hamil came again, however, Mr. Belmain had some excuse for postponing the payment a second time. Still the farmer thought his money safe in the hands of a man doing so large a business, and went home cheerful without it.

But poor Rodney, feeling that he was the means of inducing the good man to sell his crops to the hotel, began to feel very anxious. His memory was beginning to serve him in ways which were not very comfortable to himself. While he kept track of those who owed Mr. Belmain, he also took note of others whom Mr. Belmain owed. The first were

easily induced to pay ; but it seemed that Mr. Belmain never paid.   He had not paid for the clothes
Rodney wore.   He did not even pay Rodney's wages.

"He clothes and feeds me at other peoples' expense, and then keeps all the money I earn or save
for him in his own pocket!" thought the boy, growing
very indignant.   But Farmer Hamil's unpaid debt
troubled him more than all.

His suspicions once awakened, his faculty of observing everything served him well.   After winter
had set in, the hotel business became comparatively
dull, and he noticed some movements on the part of
the landlord which boded that gentleman's creditors
no good.

He urged the payment of his own wages, and
being a useful servant, he received a few dollars
from time to time.   He made no complaints, and
meanwhile kept his own counsel.

One day the farmer, who had been relying upon
his crop of hay for means to pay the interest of a
mortgage on his farm, came to Rodney in great
distress of mind, declaring that he did not know
what he was to do.

"There's no use in sueing him, for I find he don't
own anything the law can lay a finger on.   He don't
even own the horses and cows that have eaten up my
hay!"

"No, don't think of suing yet," said Rodney,
"but keep quiet, and you shall be paid."

"Are you sure?" said Farmer Hamil eagerly.

"Quite sure, if you will do as I say, and pretty soon too."

A few evenings later Mr. Belmain was busy arranging some papers in his private office, when Rodney entered.

" Be quick ! " said Mr. Belmain impatiently. " What's wanting ? "

Contact with the world in his new position had worn off the " gawkiness " in Rodney's appearance, and he stood before his employer firm and dignified.

" It's the same old want, Mr. Belmain. I want my wages. Mr. Hamil wants his pay."

"I'll pay you both to-morrow. I'm making my arrangements now,"

" I know what your arrangements are, Mr. Belmain. To-morrow will be too late — for us."

"What do you mean ? " said the landlord angrily.

" I mean that your trunk is packed, and you have a ticket for St. Louis in your pocket now."

Mr. Belmain changed color. "Don't speak so loud. Those two men out there will hear."

"They will hear nothing but the truth from me," replied Rodney. " You have plenty of money in that little black bag in the safe there ; and before you step on the train with it, there are a good many bills that ought to be paid."

"Who are you, to talk to me in this way ? " said Belmain, in a low, fierce tone, rising to his feet.

" I am a boy with a memory," Rodney replied, stepping backward towards the open door, but still

facing his employer. "I have remembered all the
people you owe, as well as those who have owed you.
I never forget a face. I saw yours for the first time
eight years ago. You were not Mr. Belmain then."

The landlord grew pale. "Come in! shut the
door!" he said, glancing out anxiously at the two
men in the hall. "This is nonsense you are talking!
When and where did you ever see me?"

"On the night of the 9th of April, between one
and two o'clock, eight years ago, when you and two
other men robbed the bank at" —

"'Sh!" hissed the landlord, with a quick movement of alarm. "You are crazy!"

"I am not so crazy but that I remember what
happened that night," said Rodney, speaking firmly.
"The cashier was my uncle. I lived in his family
then. I was awakened by a noise, and saw a light
and three men with masks on. They had bound my
uncle and aunt, and stuffed towels in their mouths,
and then they bound me. But the mask of one of
them fell off. I saw his face. He had no beard,
and there was a mole on his right cheek. If any
man doubts what I say, he may satisfy himself · by
having your whiskers shaved off. He will find a
mole on your right cheek, Mr. Belmain."

So saying, the boy who never forgot a face, looked
steadily into that of the pale and excited landlord.

"Rodney, I've always used you well, and always
meant to," said Mr. Belmain huskily, trying to
smile, "and I can't understand why you should get
up such a story as this."

"It is no story of my getting up," said Rodney. "You put on your mask, and stayed to keep guard over the rest of the family, while the other two robbers took my uncle to the bank, and, with a pistol at his head, made him open the bolts for them. He never got over it. He could never hold up his head in that town afterwards. He moved to the West, and brought me with him. He died six years ago, leaving his family poor. I was looking for honest work when you offered me a place. I didn't like you or your money. But I thought you might be trying to lead an honest life, and make up for your bad deeds, and, if so, I would give you a chance. But you" —

"Rodney," Mr. Belmain interrupted him, "I deny everything you say! It is all a wild hallucination on your part! But I — I will satisfy you. I'll pay every bill in the morning."

"Not if you take the midnight train to St. Louis, as you intend to do," replied Rodney. "Pay to-night!"

"I'll pay you and Mr. Hamil to-night."

"Very well. Here is his bill receipted."

The landlord opened his pocket-book and counted out the money.

"Now," said Rodney, as he took it, "there's plenty more in that bag in the safe; and it would save trouble if you gave it to me to pay those other bills. You know you can trust me."

"Rodney," said Mr. Belmain, "I thought you

would not ask any more. It will ruin me to pay all these. I can't and won't!"

"Well, I didn't expect you would," said Rodney. "And I don't suppose it will make much difference. Those two men out there haven't overheard much of our talk, but they know my business with you. Mr. Belmain, I am sorry I had to do it."

At a signal from Rodney, the two men advanced. One was a detective from St. Louis, the other was an officer from the town in Massachusetts where the bank robbery had been committed eight years before.

The landlord was taken into custody, and his little black bag secured. In it was found a large amount of ready money, together with government bonds, which afterwards went to satisfy the claims of those he had wronged.

The rogue himself was conveyed to Massachusetts, tried for the bank robbery, and convicted, chiefly with evidence given by Rodney Hobart. This was corroborated by several curious circumstances, one of which was the discovery of a mole on Mr. Belmain's right cheek, after his side-whiskers had been removed.

But there was one thing which the boy with the wonderful memory did seem to have forgotten. This was a reward of five hundred dollars, that had been offered at the time of the robbery for information which might lead to the conviction of either of the robbers. He was quite surprised to

learn that this reward belonged to him.   He declared
that he could never accept money earned in that way.
He took it, however, and gave it all to the impover-
ished family of his late uncle, the unfortunate cashier.

Rodney is now a prosperous young man of business
in the thriving Western town which he entered that
morning in his short trousers, with his little bundle
under his arm.   I have only to add that this story is
not one of my own invention, but that I have given
it as nearly as possible as it was given to me.

NED LIFKIN'S FOREFINGER

CHAPTER I

ROUND THE CAMP–FIRE

THEY were sitting around their ᴖcamp-fire, — five or six civil engineers and chain-bearers, — when one of them said, —

"What ever became of your forefinger, Ned?"

"Oh, that?" said Ned, with a queer look.

He stretched out his long arm, holding up the stump of the first finger of his left hand, in the firelight, and showing where it had been taken off at the middle joint.

"No, not *that*, but the part that's gone!" said his comrade. "I've often wanted to ask you about it, but didn't feel quite well enough acquainted."

"Well, boys," replied Ned, with a laugh, "after young fellows have been tramping and camping together as long as we have on this surveying expedition, in a wild country like this, it seems to me they ought to feel well enough acquainted to ask each other any familiar little question of that sort. And

I don't mind telling you that I gave my missing forefinger " — he wagged the stump in the light of the
camp-fire and looked around on his companions —
" for an education."

" Gave your forefinger for an education ! " said
another of the party.   " That's as clear as mud ! that
explains it beautifully ! "

" But I should like to know," resumed the first
speaker, " just how a fellow *can* swap off a finger in
that way, receiving a good education in return ; for
you seem to be tolerably well educated, Ned, especially in the civil-engineering line."

" Well, stir up the fire a little, Tom," said Ned,
" and I'll gratify your curiosity."

The fire was stirred, fresh bark and sticks were
flung on, the flames shot up, lighting the surrounding woods, and Ned began his story.

CHAPTER II

" A NONSENSE SHOW "

"You see, I was a poor boy; my parents were dead, and I went to live with my uncle, Joseph Lifkin, when I was sixteen years old. He is a well-to-do dairy farmer out of Lockport, in Western New York. A good sort of man ; upright, sensible, and all that, but tight as the bark of a tree, and pretty hard-headed on some points.

" ' I hope ye hain't got no foolish notions in your head,' he said to me almost the first thing after I entered his house, the first Saturday night when I went to live with him.

" ' I hope not,' I said. ' I expect to work for my living, and I don't care how soon I begin.'

" ' That's right, that's right,' said he. ' That's the way to talk. We all have to work here, Edward.'

" ' But I hope,' I continued, ' that I shall have a little time for my studies ; for I hear that there is a first-rate school here in town.'

" ' Yes, fust-best,' said he ; ' but what's that to you ? You're sixteen years old ; you've mastered the common branches ; you can read, write, and cipher, and what more does a farmer's boy want ? '

"'I should like a good deal more if I could get it,'
I replied. 'If I could go to school a part of the year,
and work to pay for my board'—

"'Well!' he interrupted me, 'I call that a foolish
notion to begin with. Why can't you be contented to
buckle down to work as I have done all my life?
You can have two or three months' schooling next
winter, if that will suit you. I can't see what you
want of any more.'

"I said I would try to be contented with what I
could get. But I soon found what *hard work* meant
on that farm! I had hoped to get time to study at
odd spells during the summer; but even if I got
the time, I was so tired, especially when evening
came, that I would fall asleep as soon as I tried to
fix my mind on my books.

"I made the most of my winter schooling; but
that wasn't much, hard as I had to work nights and
mornings about the place. I had seven or eight cows
to milk; and as three or four more were coming in
some time in February, Uncle Joe said he didn't see
but that I would have to leave school and drive the
milk-wagon.

"I was growing discouraged. 'No use trying to
get an education,' I said, and began to neglect the
studies which I couldn't do justice to.

"It was in February. I was to leave school in a
few days, when, going home one afternoon, I was
reminded by the boys that Signor Menzo was to give
three exhibitions in town during the week, beginning
that same evening.

"He had appeared there before, and left a brilliant reputation for his feats of ventriloquism and leger-demain. The boys were all going to see him, and I caught the excitement.

"I was afraid Uncle Joe would think this another of my foolish notions; so I hinted my intention to him very carefully. It was as I expected.

"'The idea of payin' out your money to see a nonsense-show like that!' he exclaimed, contemptu-ously. 'I thought you wanted to save your money for an education.'

"'I find there isn't much use in that,' I replied. I let him think, however, that I had given up seeing Signor Menzo.

"But I hadn't. I had money enough in my pocket to pay my admission-fee; and slipping out of the house after supper, I made haste to call for some other boys by the way, and went with them to the hall.

"We were in good season, and got good seats. The house was crowded, and the signor was delight-ful. I had never seen anything of the kind before, and I gave myself up to the unalloyed enjoyment of his amusing tricks.

"My spirits were dashed a little, however, when calling for an assistant out of the audience, he se-lected me.

"I occupied a seat next to the aisle and near the platform. I stood up, because he told me to; and finally walked out in front of the audience.

"But I was terribly embarrassed. I really thought it would be fun to assist the signor; but I hadn't meant that Uncle Job should know that I went to the exhibition, and I was sorry to be made conspicuous. Moreover, I was diffident, and a good deal — what shall I say?

"Well, the truth is," Ned Lifkin went on, laughing good-humoredly, "I was probably the most awkward, ungainly chap in that audience; and that, probably, was the reason why the signor chose me.

"Although only seventeen years old, I was six feet tall, with limbs extraordinarily long in proportion to my body. Just the figure for him to play off his tricks upon! A titter of laughter from my acquaintances greeted me as I went forward.

"'I am pleased to see,' said the signor, — who was no *signor* at all, but spoke English like the native-born Yankee he was, — 'that this young man is known to some of you. It will not be suspected that he is a confederate of my own. Did you ever see me before, my young friend?'

"'Never till this evening,' I replied.

"'Never till this evening,' he repeated after me, in a louder voice. 'But I shall hope for a better acquaintance. Now, my young friend, if you please, examine this box, and show it to the audience.'

"It was a plain little wooden box with a hinged cover and lock and key. Grinning bashfully, I held it up with my long arms, and showed the audience that it was empty.

"The signor then told me to lock it ; which I did, and gave him the key. Then he told me to hold it on the top of my head, where everybody could see it, and hold it tight, for he was going to drive, by force of magic, some bullets into it, and if the force of the magic was too great, they might knock the box over upon the audience.

"He then counted out six bullets, which he put under my hat on the table. He then came and placed me in a little different position, pressed my hands on the box, to make sure, he said, that his magic might not carry it away ; stepped back, and touched the hat with his wand.

"He touched it once and I could distinctly hear a bullet drop into the box. Another touch, and another bullet fell into it. And so on, till the six bullets had all been transferred from under the hat on the table into the locked box.

"People in the audience heard them drop ; and everybody, I guess, heard them rattle, when I took the box off my head and shook it, under the signor's directions. Then he gave me the key, and I unlocked the box, and there were the six bullets!"

"Six bullets, but not *the* six bullets," said one of the young men around the camp-fire.

"Perhaps not," replied Ned. "I don't pretend to explain the signor's tricks. And there's no use of describing any more of them, until he came to the trick in which I — for certain reasons — became particularly interested. That was the gun-trick

" He said any persons in the audience might see
the gun loaded and mark the bullet which he would
drop into it ; then one might fire the bullet at him
from the opposite end of the platform, and he would
catch it. ' You know about a gun ? ' he said to me.

" ' I know enough to load and fire one,' I replied.

" ' Very well,' he said. ' The audience has confidence in you ; and that they may be sure there is no
trickery in this performance, I will get you to put in
the charge.'

" He handed me the gun — a very ordinary-looking
single-barrelled fowling-piece, with an old-fashioned
percussion-cap lock. Having put on a cap, he made
me hold my hand while he poured some powder into
it from a flask.

" ' Nobody will doubt but that this is real powder
before we get through,' he said ; ' but I want you to
look at it. Does it look like powder ? '

" ' Very much like powder,' I said.

" ' Then pour it into the gun. So far so good.
Now for a wad. This will do.' He handed me a
fragment of newspaper. ' Ram that down, and remember the old adage : —

> " ' Ram your powder, not your lead,
> And you'll be sure to kill dead.' "

" I pulled the ramrod out of its sheath, and pressed
down the load with it. Then he asked one of half-a-
dozen spectators who had come upon the platform to
mark a bullet so that they would all know it again.

"The bullet was marked, and the signor called upon the entire audience to look sharply, and listen intently, while he dropped it into the gun. We saw the bullet go in — I myself holding the gun — and heard it rattle down the barrel. Then I rammed down another wad.

CHAPTER III

THE GUN TRICK

"I WAS about to return the ramrod to its place, when the signor relieved me of it and laid it on the table. I understood that movement a little later.

"'Now,' said he, 'the other gentlemen will please retire from the platform, while my young friend here shoots that bullet for me to catch. Are you a good shot?'"

"'Tolerably good,' I replied, beginning to enjoy my part in the performance, although I had been made to appear sometimes very ridiculous, especially when the signor had played off some of his feats of ventriloquism on me, and I had seemed to utter the most absurd remarks, while I had not, in fact, opened my lips. You have all witnessed tricks of that kind.

"'Very well,' said he, 'you needn't be a very exact marksman, for I can catch the bullet if it comes within my reach. But you must be careful and not shoot the audience. That would be a sorry return for their kindness.'

"'I won't do that,' I replied, in the midst of a general laugh at the bare suggestion of my making so bad a shot. 'But are you in earnest? Do you really mean that I am to shoot at you?'

" 'Certainly,' said he; 'I can't catch the bullet unless you do.'

"To tell the truth, having seen the gun loaded, and being positive that real powder and lead had gone into it, I was afraid to shoot at him — afraid of seeing him fall dead on the platform before me if I aimed the barrel as well as I knew how.

"But, reflecting that there must be some trick about it, I resolved not to draw back, and get laughed at for my weakness. I let him place me on the side of the platform, and held the gun to my shoulder in exact accordance with his instructions.

" 'Now don't move from that attitude,' he said, backing off from me. 'Don't move hand or foot, except to get a good aim exactly at the diamond-pin in my shirt-front here. That's the place I like to have a bullet start for, if I'm to catch it gracefully.'

" 'Signor,' said I, growing excited, 'if your gun is true, I can damage that diamond-pin for you, so that you will never ask another man to fire at it!'

" 'No doubt,' he replied gayly, 'unless I intercept the bullet, as I intend to do by catching it.'

"He had got his position, about eight or nine paces from me, on the opposite side of the platform.

" 'Now,' said he, 'when I give the signal — *one, two, fire!* — pull the trigger at the last word. Don't flinch!' And he held his hands as if to catch an apple about to be flung at him.

"He kept his eyes fixed upon me with keenest expression, and cried out, '*One, two, fire !*'

"I fired. The gun went off with a loud report, and for a moment I couldn't see the signor for the cloud of smoke before my eyes. Then there was a burst of applause, as he stepped forward to the centre of the stage, bowing and smiling at the audience, and holding up, between his thumb and forefinger, the marked bullet.

"Meanwhile, I was becoming conscious that something had happened to *my* forefinger which wasn't so pleasant. Blood was spurting from it, and only some ragged flesh was left in place of the first two joints.

"The signor was at my side in a moment, wrapping a handkerchief tightly about the wound. 'Say nothing !' said he in a low voice. 'But run to a surgeon as fast as you can. Why did you move your hand ? I charged you not to !'

"My brain, like my finger, had been benumbed at first. But with the pain of the hurt, my wits came to me, and I saw what had happened.

"He had been very particular, as I said, to place my hands on the gun as I held it, and I had not really intended to move them. But my arms were long for the attitude he gave me, especially my left arm ; and just before pulling the trigger, I, without thinking what I did, slipped my hand farther up the barrel. That brought my finger over the hole made apparently for the ramrod, as in other guns.

" But in *this* gun — constructed expressly for a juggler's gun — the ramrod-sheath was the actual and only bore that communicated with the vent or percussion ! It had been previously loaded with nothing but powder, and a light load, of course ; and the report was to make the spectators believe that the chamber containing the bullet had been discharged.

" But that was a false chamber, and the bullet — not the marked bullet, but one the signor had adroitly substituted for it — remained in the gun, to be afterwards withdrawn at his leisure ; while the explosion of powder in the ramrod-chamber had carried away my finger. So much for having extraordinarily long arms.

" But the thing could not be hushed up as readily as the signor supposed. ' I can't find a surgeon outside of this hall anywhere !' I exclaimed, in my fright and pain. ' Doctors and everybody are *here !* '

" Signor Menzo stepped to the front again.

" ' A slight accident to the boy, who failed to carry out my instructions,' he said blandly. ' Nothing serious. But if there is a surgeon in the audience, he'll oblige me by coming up on the platform.'

" Two doctors advanced. Somebody else advanced, too, whom I wasn't glad to see.

" One of my first thoughts, on seeing that I had really lost a finger, was, ' *Uncle Joe will have to know it all now !* ' He knew it sooner than I expected.

"It appeared that he had been as anxious that *I* shouldn't suspect *he* intended to visit the nonsense-show, as I had been to keep my little secret from him. But there he was all the time, with his hat over his eyes, in a corner, while I was made a public spectacle. The accident drew him out of his obscurity; he came forward with the doctors, and entered with us the signor's retiring-room behind the stage.

CHAPTER IV

THE FOREFINGER IS PAID FOR

"INSTEAD of upbraiding me on the spot, as I expected he would, he looked at my finger-stump, which one of the doctors removed the signor's handkerchief from, and then turned wrathfully upon the signor himself.

"'This is a sorry job for you, sir!' he cried out. 'You'll have it to pay for, and it'll cost you — it'll cost you dear!'

"'Certainly, I'll pay damages,' the signor hastened to say, no doubt having in view the harvest of his next two advertised nights. 'Don't make a noise about it. Are you the boy's father?'

"'No, but I'm his uncle and guardian, and I'm bound to see that he has justice.'

"'To be sure. What do you call justice?'

"'Well,' said my uncle hesitatingly, as if casting up accounts in his head, 'there'll be the doctors' bills, and the expense of keepin' on him while he ain't able to do chores with a finger like that, and — say fifty — seventy — a hundred dollars!'

"And my uncle put on a tremendous look, as if aware that he had named an enormous figure and meant to stand by it.

"'Very good!' said the signor cheerfully. 'What does the boy say?'

"Before I could reply, a voice‑I very well knew replied for me.

"'He says — or he will say, when he comes to reflect upon it — that a hundred dollars is no pay at all for an accident like that, which you alone are responsible for, Signor Menzo. You can well afford to pay ten times that; for here you are making a hundred dollars a night, while he will be laid up for weeks with his injury, and never have but three whole fingers on that hand. What he must have, signor, is a thousand dollars.'

"The man who said this was my teacher, and a warm friend of mine, Mr. Martin. I don't suppose he really expected to get a thousand dollars for me, though he insisted afterwards, as he did then, that it wouldn't have been a cent too much. But he meant to open the signor's eyes a little, and my uncle's too, by stating my side of the question clearly and strongly.

"The signor declared that he would stand a lawsuit before he would pay any such sum as that. Mr. Martin reminded him that the trouble and loss of public patronage which such a suit would cause him would equal many thousand dollars.

"'I know more about that than you can tell me,' the signor replied. 'I'll see you again presently. My audience is growing impatient.'

"As it was found necessary to amputate my fin-

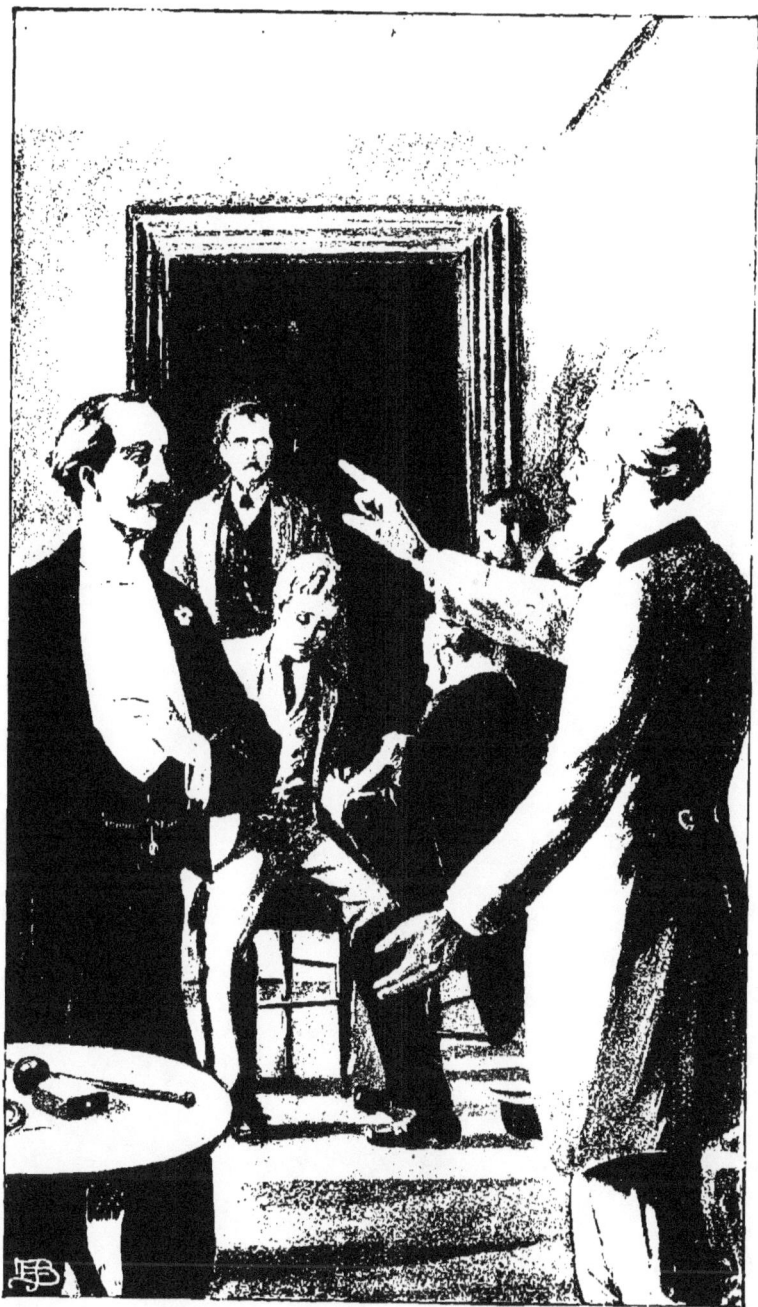

"A HUNDRED DOLLARS." — Page 179.

ger at the joint, I went off with the doctors, leaving
my uncle Joe and my friend Mr. Martin to settle
with the signor.

"Well, he was a pretty fair sort of man, and he
finally compromised the matter by paying four hundred and fifty dollars for my lost finger. I was more
than satisfied with that, I was overjoyed; though
Uncle Joe humbly admitted that we might have got
more if we had let Mr. Martin have his way.

"'But four hundred and fifty dollars is such a pile
of money!' said he, when he brought it from the
signor's hotel, after the performance. 'What under
the sun will you do with it?'

"I soon showed him what I would do with it.
My disabled hand, and the small fortune that had
fallen to me — well, boys, I see that you anticipate
me.

"I did *not* leave school that February, nor indeed
that term at all. And when I did leave it, I did so
only to eke out my means by teaching a country
school in the intervals of my studies. For, though
the lost finger did not pay all my expenses, I really
owe to it — as I told you in the first place — my
education."

FAY LIPPITT'S FOURTH OF JULY

CHAPTER I

A BILL TO COLLECT

"Now, boys," said Mr. Croswick (of Croswick, Todd & Co.), "to-morrow is the Fourth, and here's a dollar for each of you. In return for which"—

He paused, in order to enjoy the surprise and pleasure with which his munificence was received. For munificence it truly seemed to Horace Romer and Fay Lippitt, who had never before had quite so much spending-money all at once.

They were the "boys;" bright, ambitious young lads of fifteen and sixteen, who had entered the service of the firm a short time before, and had shown an equal willingness to work hard for small pay — and promotion.

"In return for which," Mr. Croswick went on with a smile, — having fully got back his money's worth in witnessing the delight with which they pocketed their dollars, — "in return for which, here's a little matter of business I'd like to have you attend to."

Horace thereupon stepped eagerly in advance of Fay, and reached out his hand for a paper Mr. Croswick held. He wished to show how ready he was to perform the required service. He also wished to forestall his companion, whom he could never see preferred before him in any matter, without a jealous pang.

As for Fay, his face shone with no less zeal to serve; but being half a year younger than Horace, he thought it right that Horace should, if he chose, accept the chief responsibility.

"You will go to town to-morrow, like most of our boys who have any money to spend," Mr. Croswick continued, still holding the paper. "It won't be asking too much of you, I think, if I request you to call on Mr. Hurd, who lives, you know, on River Street. He owes us twenty-five dollars. He will be at home to-morrow, and as he is often away, will be glad the bill is sent, even on a holiday, that he may pay it. Here it is, receipted. Of course you will bring it back if he doesn't pay it. If he does, you will bring me the money."

So saying he reached over Horace's shoulder, and gave the paper to Fay.

"Do you mean for *me* to take charge of it?" said Fay, surprised, while Horace looked as if he had been struck.

"Yes; but of course Horace will be with you. Here are tickets for the boat."

Then with some final instructions in regard to collecting the bill and taking care of the money, Mr. Croswick dismissed them.

"Isn't it grand!" Fay exclaimed, in high spirits, as they left the counting-room together.

"I don't see anything very grand about it," Horace muttered moodily. "And I don't see the use of my going with you to-morrow. Though I suppose I shall have to."

"What do you mean?" said Fay, looking at him in astonishment. "Are you angry because he gave the bill to me instead of you? He couldn't give it to both of us."

"That's all right!" said Horace, while his gloomy brow said it was all wrong. "But I was reaching for the bill, and I don't know why he shouldn't trust me as much as he does you."

"He does; of course he does!" Fay protested, trying to soothe his friend's wounded feelings. "Don't spoil it all now!"

"Well, I won't," said Horace, beginning to be ashamed of his foolish envy, and resolving to conceal if he could not conquer it.

He had come out of his cloud when the two met the next morning and set off together for the day's excursion.

The ride down the river and across the bay was delightful. They found on board the steamboat several boys they knew; and all on landing went together to the park, where they enjoyed the noise and excitement of a Fourth of July in the city as only boys can.

But the business with which he had been entrusted was on Fay's mind. Horace showed little interest in it ; and it was only when Fay, after urging him in vain, was actually setting off without him to see Mr. Hurd, that he finally consented to leave their companions and accompany him.

"Because," as he said, "I suppose you will tell Mr. Croswick if I don't."

"I don't see why I should tell him," said Fay. "Only, you know, he said you were to go with me."

CHAPTER II

UP IN A BALLOON

THEY found Mr. Hurd at home; and he paid the bill in bank-notes, which Fay received and counted with a cool air of business that made the heart of Horace burn in his bosom. That he, the older of the two, should thus sit by and see the other manage the matter so independently, was to him a bitter humiliation.

Mr. Hurd gave Fay an envelope in which to place the money; which done, Fay put it carefully in his inside breast-pocket. Warm as the day was, he buttoned his coat over the precious package on going out.

They returned to the sports in the park; treated themselves at the booths, shot at the targets with Indian bows and air-guns, and tried the lifting-machine to see how much they could lift, and the breathing-machine to see which had the biggest breath; saw the puppet-show, and the panorama, and the regatta, and having eaten a sandwich or two, and drank lemonade, and stuffed their pockets with peanuts, each had half-a-dollar of his own money, or Mr. Croswick's gift, and one great and glorious pleasure left.

The balloon !

They did not think of going up in it at first. But other boys who had had that experience assured them that it was worth everything else that this or any other Fourth of July could show.

"I will, if you will!" said Horace, who, having beaten Fay at lifting and breathing and shooting, was now in an amiable mood again.

"I will, if you will!" said Fay, glad enough to have made his companion good-natured at so slight a cost.

"Come on!" said Horace.

The balloon was surrounded by a pretty constant crowd of spectators, kept back from it by an enclosure, within which any person was admitted on the payment of fifty cents. That entitled him to an aërial voyage to the extent of I know not how many hundred feet of rope.

"I've always wondered how it would seem to go up in a balloon!" said Fay, in a tremor of excitement as they paid the fee and went in.

"It will be worth a good deal more than half-a-dollar just to *say* we have been up in one!" was Horace's way of looking at it.

One end of the rope was attached to the aërial car, and the other to a windlass, which let it out rapidly as the balloon went up, and wound it slowly to bring it down again.

"Is there any danger of its getting away?" Fay inquired, as he and Horace mounted the platform against which the car was held fast.

"Not the least, not the least in the world," said one of the men in charge. "Step aboard! Take your seats on opposite sides, so as to balance the car. All ready! Now keep your seats, young gentlemen, and *bon voyage !*"

The boys were in a flutter of expectation, with just enough of nervous apprehension in it to give zest to their delight.

There was indeed little danger of the rope's breaking; but if they had known what an old balloon it was, or what a strain was just then put upon it by the intense heat of the afternoon sun expanding the gas within and rarefying the air without, they might have had fears of a different catastrophe.

The word was given, the windlass whirled, out flew the rope, and up went the balloon. Higher! higher! the two boys and the handkerchiefs they waved over the sides of the car growing rapidly less and less to the sight of those below. Then the brake was put on, and the speed of the ascent gradually slackened.

Meanwhile, how describe the sensations of the two voyagers mounting into the blue? It seemed almost as if the planet were suddenly dropping away from under them and was sinking into space.

The crowd below, the park with its booths and groups, the city itself with its squares and streets and wharves, receded swiftly and became reduced to a map, while the world expanded around.

"See the little steamboats down there in the bay!" said Horace.

"And the villages all about! I do believe we can see *our* village off there!" exclaimed Fay.

"If our folks only knew!" said Horace, to whom the glory of the thing was even more than the thing itself.

"I'm glad my mother won't know till I get safe home and tell her about it," replied Fay. "Wouldn't she be frightened?"

"Of course," said Horace. "Mothers are always silly!"

"I thought it was going to be cold up here," Fay remarked. "But it's just as warm!"

"I believe they're stopping us," said Horace. "It's too bad! I wish the rope was ten times as long. What's that?"

It was a strange rending sound over their heads, followed by a rushing and hissing noise. Fay turned pale.

"What can it be? I smell something!"

"Gas!" murmured Horace, with frightened lips.

"I wish they would take us down!" cried Fay. "I'll shout!"

Putting his face over the side of the car he perceived by the upward current of air that they were descending already.

"I think the balloon has burst!" said Horace.

"We are falling!" gasped Fay.

Down! down! faster! faster! strong and furious came the upward rush of air, with shouts and cries of alarm from the spectators below.

" We shall surely be killed ! " said Horace.

" Oh ! my mother ! my mother ! " said Fay.

What a sight it was to the people in the park !
The balloon shot down faster than the rope could
possibly have been wound in, even had the men at
the windlass been prepared.

At the same time the light breeze that prevailed
carried it far beyond the enclosure from which it had
risen, beyond the borders even of the park, — over
the street where carriages and horse-cars were passing.

CHAPTER III

WHAT BECAME OF THE MONEY

THE collapsed case fortunately doubled in its net-ting as the freighted basket bore it down, so that it became shaped something like an umbrella, and its descent was somewhat checked.

A murmur of horror and dismay went up from the crowd, and there was a sudden rush towards the spot where in an instant, it was expected, the two boys would fall to the ground.

But before it reached the earth the balloon made a strange halting and swaying movement, incompre-hensible to those who witnessed it at a distance.

The billowy bag had caught on a line of telegraph wires, which held it for a moment, while the car swung under, half-capsizing, and then swung back, striking the ground and throwing the boys out head-long.

There was a crowd around them in a moment, and sincere was the rejoicing when it was found that they were not killed.

They were badly shaken up, however, and Fay was for a minute quite stunned. But soon he too was on his feet, looking dazed and frightened enough, but declaring that he wasn't hurt.

"I guess we've had ballooning enough for one day," he said, with a pallid smile, as he brushed the dust from his clothes. "And Fourth of July enough too."

"I think so," said Horace, trembling with agitation. "Let's get out of this."

They had many questions to answer as they made their way out of the crowd, which gradually dispersed, while the wrecked balloon was gathered up and carried back to the enclosure in the park.

The boys felt strangely weak and tremulous when all was over, and soon tired of answering questions. They were on their way to the steamboat pier, when Fay, who had been thinking only of their wonderful escape from death, and longing to get home, put up his hand, stopped, fumbled hurriedly in his breast-pocket, and uttered a despairing cry.

"The money! O Horace! What shall I do?"

"You don't mean you've lost it?" said Horace.

"It's gone! it's gone!" said Fay, pulling out the lining of his pocket in an agony of terror.

He thought he had known what fear was when the balloon was falling. But what he felt now was something even more distressing, in a certain way, to a sensitive and high-minded boy.

Then only his life was in danger; but now his honor, his fortune, his future (as it seemed to him), were at stake.

He had lost what he regarded as a large sum of money ; and he had failed in an important trust.

"Let's go straight back where the balloon fell," said Horace. "Though if you lost it there, some-body must have picked it up."

"Of course I lost it there," said Fay. "And any-body that picked it up must know it belonged to one of us."

"You may have had your pocket picked before that," replied Horace. "*I* shouldn't have been willing to carry so much money about with me, in a crowded park, as *you* did."

If this was not intended as a reproach, it was yet so different from the consolation he needed, and had a right to expect from a friend, that Fay quite gave up, and almost sobbed with despair and grief, as they turned to retrace their steps.

"What else could I do?" he asked.

"You needn't have been in such a hurry to get the money. You might have waited till just before we started for home. That's the way *I* should have done," said Horace, "if *I* had had charge of the business."

"I went early, so I could go again if I didn't find Mr. Hurd the first time. And you never told me you thought there was danger I might be robbed of the money!"

"If I had said that, you would have thought it was because *I* wanted to have charge of it. But you felt so grand, I saw it was no use for me to say a word."

"O Horace!" Fay moaned, at these unfeeling words. "How can you?"

"I'm only telling you what's true," said Horace. "But I'm going to help you all the same. Maybe we can find the money. Anyhow, I wouldn't blubber like that, whether we find it or not."

Fay dried his eyes, and repressed his sobs, and hastened back with his friend to the spot under the dislocated and sagging telegraph wires which told where the balloon had fallen.

But of course no package of money was to be found in a place so public, traversed by throngs of people. And the boys inquired for it in vain.

Search was indeed useless; yet Fay could not endure the thought of going home without it.

"I'd rather die," he said, "than meet Mr. Croswick — and my mother — and tell them" —

"Don't feel so!" said Horace. "Come, we've only just time to get the boat!"

But it was all he could do to drag the wretched boy away.

Half an hour later Fay was sitting on a stool under the steamboat awning, lonely, disconsolate, with a great bump on his forehead, his eyes red, his cheeks pale; while Horace, weary of his miserable company, walked about or sat with other boys, and talked of his ballooning adventure. Fay could not bear to talk of it with anybody.

All at once he stepped to Horace's side, and remained near him during the remainder of the voyage.   He said little, but kept his eyes on him with a desperate, determined look, which Horace could not understand.

On landing, at twilight, they walked up the street together; Fay silent and morose, and Horace vainly endeavoring to make sympathizing and friendly talk. Fay did not answer, until Horace proposed to leave him on a corner.

"No, sir!" said Fay resolutely. "You are going with me to Mr. Croswick's."

"What good will that do?" asked Horace uneasily. "You haven't got the money."

"But I am going to see him all the same.   And you are going too."

"I don't see the use."

"You will see by-and-by.   Come along!"

Fay's manner was so strange that Horace wondered at it more and more, and felt exceedingly uncomfortable as he went with him a little way down the dusky street.

Then he held back again.

"I *won't* go to-night!" he exclaimed.

"Then you will do another thing!" said Fay, seizing him by the arm, and confronting him with blazing eyes.

"What's that?" cried Horace, backing against the fence.

"You know well enough," said Fay, in a low voice. "Give me that money!"

"What do you mean?" said Horace.

"Give me that money!" Fay repeated. "You've got it! I know you've got it!"

Horace tried to hold him off with one hand, while with the other he reached around, as if to steady himself against the fence.

"How should I have it?" he cried. "Don't be a fool! I *haven't* got the money!"

"Go with me to Mr. Croswick, and tell him so! Let him search you in my presence. Then I'll believe you."

"I'll go with you," said Horace, pale and agitated. "Only tell me what has put such a strange notion into your head."

"I'll tell you when we get to Mr. Croswick's," said Fay.

"Tell me first, or I won't go!"

"Very well, then, I'll tell you. Mr. Hobson came to me when I was alone on the steamboat, and said that before I came to myself, after we fell out of the balloon, he saw a stranger pick up a package in a yellow envelope that had dropped out of one of our pockets, and hand it to *you!* So I know you have had it; and I believe you have got it yet. What's that?"

Horace had dropped something behind him, through an opening in the fence. In an instant Fay looked over, reached through, and had the precious package in his hand.

He merely looked to see that the seal was unbroken, then thrust it back into his own pocket, and

once more buttoned his coat over it.   He said noth-
.ing, but his whole countenance gleamed.

Horace stood in a stupor of fear and bewilderment until he saw him starting off.   Then he called
after him imploringly, —

" Don't tell Mr. Croswick ! "

" Why shouldn't I tell Mr. Croswick ? "

" I didn't mean any wrong !   I wasn't going to
steal the money !   I was only going to hand it to
Mr. Croswick."

" How could you be so mean, so cruel to *me* ? "
Fay demanded.

" I was angry because he trusted you," Horace
confessed ; " and I had been wishing something
would happen to make him sorry he hadn't trusted
me instead.   Then the man gave me the package.
I thought I would keep it for awhile, and pretend
afterwards I didn't know, in the confusion, it had
been given to me.   Then when you felt so bad,
I wanted to let you know ; but the longer I kept it
the harder it was to explain " —

" O Horace ! Horace ! " was all Fay Lippitt could
say.

" Must you tell Mr. Croswick ? " Horace asked.

" No ; I think you have told me the truth — and
it isn't necessary that I should tell him."

Fay kept his word.   He handed the money to Mr.
Croswick, saw him count it, said he had had a *pretty*
good time, spoke carelessly of the rather too rapid
descent of the balloon, to account for the bunch on

his forehead, and then ran home to his mother. It was a comfort to tell her all.

Whether Mr. Croswick heard of Horace's unworthy conduct from other sources, I cannot say. He was a sagacious, observant man ; and he did not need that knowledge to teach him which of the two boys was the more worthy of trust.

THE BAMBERRY BOYS AND THEIR FLOCK OF SHEEP

CHAPTER I

HOW THEY CAME BY THE FLOCK

THERE were five of the Bamberry boys; and when the oldest of them (Burton) was seventeen, and the youngest (Johnny) was seven, their Uncle Todd, a successful wool-grower in an adjoining county, made each of them a present of a sheep.

Mr. Bamberry, the boys' father, had tried the experiment of sheep-raising a few years before, but had abandoned it, after having nearly all his flock killed by dogs.

"You never can find out whose dogs do the mischief," he said; "and it's too much trouble to keep constant watch and ward against them. No!" he would add emphatically, when his boys teased him to begin again with a few lambs, "I never want to see another sheep come upon my farm!"

But he was a good-natured man; and when Uncle Todd made his offer of five yearling lambs, provided the boys would go over after shearing-time and make him a visit and drive them home, Mr. Bamberry, reluctantly assenting, said : —

"Well, well! try it, if you will ; but remember, it's your experiment, not mine."

Then the question arose, who should go for the sheep ? and as not one of the boys was willing to remain at home, — not even seven-year-old Johnny, nor Henry, the third one, who was lame, — it was decided that they all should go. They could take Dolly and the one-horse wagon, drive over one day, and return with the sheep the next.

It was a delightful adventure ; and never were five boys happier than the Bamberry brothers when, on the second morning, while the air was yet cool and the dew on the grass, they set out with their bleating flock for home. They proceeded leisurely, letting the young sheep nibble occasionally by the wayside ; and when one appeared tired and lagged too much, they picked it up and tumbled it into the wagon. At eleven o'clock they stopped to feed the horse and eat their own luncheon at a roadside spring, and by the middle of the afternoon they arrived home triumphantly with their little flock.

Nothing interests boys on a farm so much as something of their own to take care of and hope for profit from ; and Uncle Todd's gift proved in many ways a benefit, not only to the brothers, but to the whole Bamberry household. It served to cure Burton of his restlessness ; and from that time Todd, the second son (named after his uncle), began to show an interest in farm matters, which had never had the least attraction for him before. And the flock was a bond of union between the five boys, making them not only better brothers, but better sons.

Mr. Bamberry was to have the wool in return for pasturage and fodder; but the sheep and their increase were to belong to the boys. The flock prospered, numbering eleven the second year (including two pairs of twins), and eighteen the third, not counting two or three lambs which the boys had fattened for the table and sold to their father for a good price.

As a protection against dogs, the boys had built a high pen of unplaned boards, on the edge of the pasture where the flock ranged in summer. Into this fold the sheep were enticed every evening by a little salt or a few handfuls of beans, which they learned to expect, and came for so regularly, that it was very little trouble to shut them up for the night. If not already at the wicket, when one of the young shepherds appeared at dusk, his cheery call, " Ca-day! Ca-day!" or "Nan! Nan! Nan!" would bring the sheep scampering over the hills and crowding into the enclosure. Then they were left to lick the salt or nibble at the beans in the troughs, and the wicket was shut for the night.

All went well until, one September evening of that third year, Johnny, then aged ten, went to put up the sheep. He found them already running to the pen, and he noticed that they appeared frightened.

Having pacified them with the contents of his little pail, he passed by the troughs, to see if they were all there. A count, carefully repeated, showed him that a sheep and a lamb were missing.

Then he went out and called, but heard no answering bleat, and saw no sheep or lamb coming over the shadowy slopes in the twilight. Fearing some danger to them, he ran to the summit of the hill, and looked off into the dim hollows beyond, calling " Caday ! Ca-day ! Nan ! Nan ! Come, Nan ! " as loud as he could.

Getting no response, he hurried on, looking behind stone-heaps and old stumps, and in the corners of fences, until suddenly he saw flit away before him something which he mistook for a sheep. But no ! it was a dog. It disappeared almost immediately in the darkness, and Johnny stood trembling with fear.

CHAPTER II

"ABOUT WHAT I EXPECTED"

HE immediately ran home and told his brothers, who went with pitchforks, a lantern, and a gun, to find the missing members of the flock. They were soon found, not far from the spot where Johnny had seen the dog; and two more dogs, or the same dog and another, darted away at the approach of the lantern, and disappeared before Todd could bring the gun to his shoulder.

The sheep and lamb were both dead, the mother having perhaps sacrificed her life in trying to protect her young, instead of cantering away with the rest of the frightened flock. Even if there had been no other evidence, the mangled throats of the victims betrayed that the slaughter was the work of dogs.

The boys were greatly excited; and as they dragged the slain creatures homeward, across the dreary pasture, Johnny exclaimed bitterly : —

"That was my little pet, the prettiest lamb of the whole flock!"

" I thought dogs killed sheep only at night," said Will, the fourth son, who carried the lantern.

" So did I," said Burt. "And it's a pretty pass

we've come to, if penning our sheep at night won't answer, and they can be dogged and killed before it is fairly dark, and almost under our eyes! I believe one of those curs was Judge Mason's."

"I thought one was Haniman's miserable mongrel," said Todd.

Mr. Bamberry was hardly less exasperated than the boys when they reached home with the bad news. But he said: —

"It's about what I expected. There's no way to keep sheep safe from dogs in this neighborhood, unless you watch 'em or pen 'em day and night. And now the trouble's begun, I'm afraid you'll have enough of it."

"We'll see about some of those dogs!" said Burton angrily.

"That will be of no use," said his father. "You can't trace 'em; and there'll be worse trouble if you touch any man's dog without positive proof of his guilt."

Burt whispered to Todd; and taking the lantern, they went over to call on the Haniman boys, to tell them of their loss. The Hanimans listened with interest and sympathy; but when Todd said, "I think your dog was one of them," they cried out indignantly against so absurd a suspicion.

"Our Prince?" said Joe Haniman. "Why, he's the gentlest, kindest, truest dog in the world! Here, Prince!" And he began to whistle.

"He goes with our sheep, and protects 'em," said

Joe's brother Bob. "You couldn't get him to hurt one ; if you should set him on a sheep, he would only just catch and hold it."

"You couldn't have seen him," Joe stopped whistling to say. "He's always at home ; I saw him not half an hour ago. Here, Prince ! — here he is now," as the gentlest, kindest, truest dog in the world came bounding to his side. "There ! does he look like a dog that would kill sheep ?"

He certainly did not ; and Todd was easily convinced that he had been mistaken. Prince was a long-legged, tawny mongrel, and there were perhaps fifty dogs in the county that might be taken for him in the dusk.

The Bamberry boys next went to call on Judge Mason, Burt saying that he himself had not been half so sure of the Haniman dog as he was of the judge's.

They found the judge kind and candid, but inclined to scoff at the notion that his Roland could be guilty of so grave an offence.

"Where is he now ? " Burt inquired.

"I don't know," said the judge. "He's about the place somewhere ; I saw him not ten minutes since. He may have slipped off, to avoid being shut up for the night in the woodshed ; he does sometimes. But he's the most harmless dog — you know him."

"I know him only too well," replied Burt. "And I'm confident I saw him to-night."

" Pooh ! pooh ! don't be too hasty," said the judge,

putting his hand on Burt's shoulder. "Could you swear that as a fact you really saw him?"

"No," Burt admitted; "but —

"You are not certain; and even if you did see him, that fact never would convince me that Roland had killed your sheep. Why, boys, I've such confidence in that noble dog that I'm not afraid to offer fifty dollars for every sheep killed in this county, if he can be proved to have been in any way concerned in killing or mangling one."

"It may be hard to prove. But I should like to see your dog now," said Todd.

"Well, you can see him; he can't be far away." And the judge called, but called in vain; no Roland appeared. "He's afraid of the woodshed," said his master with an indulgent laugh. "Can't blame him. That dog's very cunning!"

The boys went to the houses of two or three other neighbors who kept dogs, but got no satisfaction anywhere.

"I knew just how it would turn out," said their father, on their return home. "No man will admit that his dog kills sheep, though you should canvass the country. The only way is for one of you to keep in sight of the flock during the day, and then pen them early."

The boys resolved to act by this advice, and make the best of their misfortune. But worse was yet to come.

On the second morning after this, on going to let

out the flock, Henry was astonished by what he saw. Five sheep had been killed in the night, and lay dead in the pen with their throats mangled. The others started and huddled into corners at the slightest sound or motion, showing that they had been subjected to a recent great fright and disturbance.

CHAPTER III

THE TRAP

Henry did not open the wicket, but limped homeward as fast as he could ; and it was not long before
his brothers were with him on the spot.   For a while,
not much was to be heard but muttered vengeance.
Todd and Will were for going off at once and seek-
ing for evidence of sheep-killing among all the dogs
in town — traces of their recent feast must be discovered on some of them ; but Burt said : —

"I've tried that once; and, as father says, it's of
no use.   The best way is to keep still, and think of
some plan to get even with them."

"We must do something soon," said Todd, "or
we shall lose all our sheep, now that the brutes have
had a taste of them.   I thought this pen was high
enough, and close enough, to protect them against all
dogs, big or little."

"It must be a very small dog that could crawl
between these boards," said Henry; "and a very
long-legged one that could jump over.   I wouldn't
have believed any dog in the world could clear such
a fence ! "

"The dogs that killed those sheep certainly got

over, and I'm sure there was more than one," said Burt. "None that could crawl through would be apt to have strength or courage to attack a flock. Boys, look here!"

."Scratches, as sure as fate!" said Henry. "See here!—and here!"

Marks on the boards were found, indicating that attempts to get over had been made by dogs that had left the prints of their claws on the fence, either in leaping up or in falling back. Places, too, were discovered, where the lower ones had been clawed and gnawed, as if in efforts to get through.

"I'll tell you, boys!" cried Todd, "there's been a whole pack of dogs here! Some have got over, and the rest couldn't. Some have tried to work through."

"Sheep-killing dogs go in packs, like wolves," said Burt. "When one discovers a flock open to attack, it seems as if he went and told the others. Constant watching, after that, is the only thing that can save a single one of that flock. It is just as father has told us all along; and all the comfort we shall get out of him will be, 'It's what I expected; now maybe you'll believe what I say.' What are we going to do?"

"I believe," said Henry, "we can trap the dogs, just as I have heard of farmers trapping wolves in old times."

"I've thought of that," said Todd. "It will be better than trying to kill them off by poisoning some of the meat and leaving it for them to eat."

" Say nothing to anybody, boys," said Burt; "but let us set quietly to work, and rebuild this pen in such a way that any dog that wants to get *in* can do so without much trouble. We'll have it harder for him to get *out*, I tell you ! "

They found some comfort in talking over the plan and anticipating the results. The living sheep were let out, and the dead ones left in the pen, which before night was made considerably higher. But on the side toward the pasture, at which the dogs had evidently got over, one section of the fence was made to slant inward toward the top, so that dogs could easily run up and leap over, while it would be impossible for the " longest-shanked cur in creation," as Todd said, " to jump back again."

That evening, after having been watched by one of the boys all day, the living sheep and lambs were driven to the shed and shut in ; but the dead sheep were left in the pen, and the wicket was made fast. Then the boys withdrew, to await anxiously what might happen over night.

They feared that, dogs being probably more knowing than wolves, it might not be easy to catch them in such a trap; and then, when it was too late to go back to the pen, they began to think over and discuss all the possibilities of the marauders getting out again, even if caught. But there was nothing to be done before morning except to sleep, if they could.

They had youth and health ; and they slept, not-

"We've got 'em." — Page 213.

withstanding their excitement. But at the first streak of day, Burt and Todd were up; and their whispers, as they hurriedly dressed, in the great farm-house garret, awoke their brothers. Ten-year-old Johnny was the last to get his sleepy eyes unsealed and tumble out of bed ; and with some of his clothes on and the rest in his hands, he followed the others down the dim stairs, and out into the cool, gray September morning.

The boys looked first to see that the sheep in the shed had not been molested ; then they hastened on to the fold which they had converted into a trap. Lame Henry, whom even little Johnny outstripped in that eager race, hobbled behind ; while Todd, the best runner, was the first to reach the pen. He looked through the fence. There was a pause, and silence of a few seconds, broken only by the sounds of feet hurrying behind him. Then he turned and flung up his hands excitedly, shouting back at his brothers : —

"We've got 'em! we've got 'em! Come, quick!" He beckoned frantically, and, turning again to look into the pen, almost went into convulsions of gleeful triumph as Burt and Will and Johnny came clattering to the spot.

Then Henry, still in the rear, but watching sharply what was taking place at the pen, saw the others go into similar convulsions, as one by one they peeped between the rails ; and finally he himself followed the prevailing custom, as he came up and took a look.

CHAPTER IV

A WONDERFUL CATCH

AND well might the young owners of those slain sheep exult! Never before; I am sure, did a sheep-fold in a region rid of wild beasts present so amazing a spectacle.

Dogs! At first sight, it seemed almost full of them. There were twenty-three by actual count (and this is no fiction); dogs of nearly all colors, shapes, and sizes, known the country round: surly bull-dogs, restless fox-hounds, and meeching mongrels, with cringing tails.

There were several neighbors' dogs that the boys knew; among them, "the kindest, gentlest, truest dog that ever was," — Haniman's Prince, — and Judge Mason's "noble" Roland! There were also dogs that none of the Bamberries remembered ever to have seen before. There were even three or four half-breed shepherd dogs, that had left unhurt their own masters' flocks to prey upon the flocks of their neighbors.

"Roland was a little too cunning for his own good!" chuckled Will. "The woodshed he hates so would have been better for his health last night."

The dead sheep had been partly devoured, observing which, Todd remarked : —

" I thought dogs were more knowing than wolves ; but they say wolves, caught in such a trap, never will touch a sheep until they find a safe way out again."

There was an animated discussion as to what should be done with so many dangerous members of the community. Todd thought they ought to shoot them all, and then call upon the owners to pay damages.

" We'll have the damages," said Burt, "and I've no doubt most of the dogs deserve to be killed ; but I prefer to let the owners do the killing. Some are valuable dogs ; and it's more their masters' fault than their own that they have been allowed to run loose, and get into temptation, along with bad company. They have been simply acting out their original dog-nature."

" Yes ; but the way they act," said Todd, " shows they have some conscience about such things, and know that they have been doing wrong."

" They know they are caught, and will probably get punished ; that's all their conscience amounts to," said Will, who strongly advocated the shooting policy.

" It looks like a dog-show !" exclaimed Johnny, walking around to get a good view of all the slinking and cowering curs.

From that Burt took a hint.

"A dog-show it is, and a dog-show it shall be! We'll have some fun out of this thing, boys, and maybe some money to pay us for all our trouble and loss."

The idea became immediately popular.

"Admission, ten cents; children under twelve years old, half price," laughed Henry.

"Owners of dogs contributed, to be put on the free list," said Todd.

"'Contributed' is good!" cried Burt, with grim humor.

"So is 'free list,'" added Will. "Perhaps we'd better offer prizes!"

"That might be going a little too far; we must draw the line somewhere," observed Todd dryly. "Any owner who will come forward like a man, pay damages, and take his animal away, may see the show for nothing. How's that, boys?"

"All right," replied Burt. "But how about the damages?"

"I say, make every man that has a dog in this show pay a round ten dollars," said Will; "or else kill his dog."

"And prosecute him, under the law," added Todd. "Boys, we have control of the whole affair now."

"That's true," assented Burt. "And for that very reason we should be careful."

"Temper justice with mercy," observed Henry.

The matter was talked over with their father, who said, as he came and looked into the pen, "Well done ! well done, boys ! a good catch, a wonderful catch, I declare ! " But he objected to a part of their plan.

" It's fair and right," he said, "to make every man whose dog is found here pay a round sum for him, say, five dollars. But I'm afraid it will look a little too much like a money-making job on our part if you charge anything for admission to the show."

The boys thought he was right ; and though they were reluctant to give up that advantage, they concluded to have the fun without the profit, and make the show free to the public.

CHAPTER V

THE DOG—SHOW

AFTER breakfast, while Henry and Johnny remained to watch the captives, with a loaded gun and plenty of ammunition, Burt and Todd and Will set off on horseback, riding in different directions, to notify all owners of dogs within a radius of six or eight miles to come and claim their property; and, incidentally, they invited everybody to the show.

One of the first persons Todd called upon was Judge Mason, whom he found in his peach-orchard.

"Good-morning, Judge Mason," he said, cheerfully, from his horse. "Is your dog about the place this morning?"

"Well! — hm!" coughed the judge, "I suppose so. I think I saw him." He was not a man who would tell an untruth; and he must have imagined that he had seen Roland very recently.

"Was he shut in the woodshed last night?" Todd asked.

"I've no doubt of it; I gave orders that he should be," said the judge. "Any more trouble with your sheep?"

Instead of answering this question, Todd asked another : —

" Do you remember your offer of fifty dollars for every sheep killed in the county, if your dog was proved to have been concerned in killing or mangling one ? "

"I believe I did say that, I know Roland so well ! " exclaimed the judge. " Why ? "

" Because," said Todd, with a gleaming smile, "according to that, you owe us three hundred and fifty dollars."

" What ! what ! what ! " said the judge.

" It is no mere suspicion this time," said Todd. " If you have seen your noble and harmless dog this morning, you've seen him in the trap we set for him, where I just left him, shut up with the carcasses of five more sheep, killed night before last. That makes seven in all — three hundred and fifty dollars ! " he repeated, with a very grim sort of laugh.

" Todd Bamberry ! " said the judge positively, "it's impossible ! "

" Seeing is believing," rejoined Todd. " Won't you come over, please, and see for yourself ? "

" Then you boys caught him and put him there ! " declared the judge, looking very red and angry.

"There are twenty-two other dogs with him," said Todd. " Could we have caught them all and shut them up together ? We must have had a lively night's work if we did ! "

"Well ! well ! " said the judge, " I'm astounded. " I'll go over and see about it."

"Do, if you please. Father is waiting to talk with the owners who come to take their dogs away. We'll let the noble Roland off for a trifle less than three hundred and fifty! " And Todd galloped away.

Burt, meantime, had seen the Haniman boys, and notified them of Prince's capture. So the three went the rounds of the neighborhood, and far beyond, spreading the news, which created an extraordinary sensation, remembered to this day in all that part of the country.

The show was well patronized that afternoon, men and boys flocking from all parts to see the catch of twenty-three sheep-killers, secured by the Bamberry boys in one night. Visitors were coming and going all the afternoon; and fifteen of them led away dejected-looking curs, with tails between their legs and ropes around their necks.

At night, eight of the dogs remained unclaimed; and for five of them no owners ever appeared. They were accordingly shot. How many of the others shared the same fate, at the hands of masters who despaired of their reform, the boys never knew.

For most of the eighteen that were redeemed they received five dollars each; but for a few they got only a part, in cash, of the penalty demanded, and were never able to collect the whole. The total sum which they realized was a little over sixty-seven dollars; and that they considered sufficient to cover past damages and some future risks.

They kept their sheep-pen built in the same way, but never again caught any dogs, nor lost any more sheep from canine depredations. Their flock prospered, and their father was obliged at length to acknowledge that the experiment was a success.

NELS THURLOW'S TRIAL

CHAPTER I

A BAD LOAD OF HAY

THE last of Mr. Podlong's fine hay crop had been raked into windrows in prime condition for the mow.

There was still one load to go in when a black thunder-cloud loomed up in the western sky. Then all was hurry and worry in the hayfield. The horses returned at a gallop from the barn, driven by Dick Stark, the hired man, and the wagon, with its broad rack, went clattering over the uneven ground.

Guiding the team alongside one of the great, light, loosely tumbled windrows, Dick threw off the reins, and leaped down with his fork, while old man Podlong got down more slowly with his rake, and Nelson Thurlow, a boy of fifteen, stayed in the wagon to load and trample the hay as it was pitched on.

Dick Stark rolled up immense forkfuls, and heaved them over the side of the rack, sometimes half burying Nelson; and Mr. Podlong scratched up the leavings and trimmed the sides of the load. Even the horses

seemed to catch the spirit of work; they threw up
their heads and tossed their manes as the cool wind
blew over them in the shadow of the black cloud after
a sultry day, and started with alertness the moment
Dick touched the reins.

The "worry" was all done by old man Podlong.
Notwithstanding his years and white hair (he was
near seventy), he had an irritable and impatient temper, with but little wisdom to control it.

"Rain'll be here in five minutes," he cried.
"Hay'll git wet, sure as anything.   We *must* put
in, boys, all we know how! O Nels!" he roared
out, "what a load you're making!"

"How can the boy do any better while I'm putting
the hay on faster'n a man can take care of it in decent
shape?" cried Dick, pausing for Nels to lay out a
corner.   "If it will only ride, that's all we care for.
There's no use fretting."

"Guess *you'd* fret if 'twas *your* hay, 'stead o'
standin' there sassin' me, with your hands in your
pockets," replied the old man angrily, plying his rake
behind the load.

"Sassin' you?   My hands in my pockets?" Dick
retorted.   "I only tell you what I think of your fretting.   And as for my hands, they couldn't do more
if the hay was mine, and I thought as much of a dollar
as you do."

"Waal, waal!" said the old man, in a heat of ill-
suppressed fury, as he felt a raindrop strike his hand,
"will ye pitch on the hay, or won't ye?"

"I will when I get ready, and Nels is ready to take care on't," Dick answered.

He began to pitch again with almost too much zeal, sending up masses of hay which Nels found it impossible properly to distribute and trample, with the wind likewise tearing and tossing it.

Nels knew the old man's temper too well to say a word ; he could only hope that the hay would stay on till it got into the barn. He was struggling with it in the squall, when suddenly an accumulated heap, carried clean across the top by the force of the gale, rolled off on the other side, carrying a good corner of the load with it.

CHAPTER II

PODLONG STRIKES DICK, AND DICK STRIKES WORK

"Lucky I'm up here out of his reach," Nels said to himself, anticipating the old man's wrath. "Uncle, I couldn't help that," he cried.

Mr. Podlong looked up, and, seeing him well beyond the sweep of his rake, turned his fury upon Dick.

"You done that a-purpose," he said. And down came the brandished rake upon Dick's head.

Dick's coarse felt hat was a protection, and his head was not badly hurt, though his pride was. He felt for a moment as if he would like to take the old man on his fork, and "pitch him into the middle of next week," as he afterward expressed it ; and Nels, peering over the side of the load, looked to see a bloody battle.

But Dick simply threw down the fork, and adjusted his hat. "That ends my work for you," he said.

"You leave this hay in the rain?" yelled the old man.

"I leave it and you," Dick replied with determination.

"But you hired to me for the summer," Podlong remonstrated, lifting his rake again.

"What did I hire for?" said Dick. "To work the best I knew how, as I've done, and as I've been ready to do, up to this minute; Nels will bear me out in that. But I don't hire out to anybody to stand and have rakes broken over my head. Don't you hit me again, old man!"

"Then go to work. The rain is coming," said Podlong, half threatening, half imploring.

"I wouldn't do another stroke for you if Noah's deluge was coming," returned Dick. "I've no more business with you, except to get my pay."

"And that you never will get, without you clap to and help us with this load into the barn. Not a cent, if it costs me my farm to keep you out of it," the old man declared.

"We'll see," muttered Dick, turning to walk away. "You, Nels, will bear witness to his striking me."

Nels had seen and heard the blow, and he could not blame Dick in the least. But, foreseeing trouble, and fearing the old man's anger, he did not open his mouth.

Uncle Podlong took up the fork Dick had dropped, and set out to throw on a little more of the hay. But his limbs shook so with excitement and the feebleness of age that he soon gave up the attempt, and, reaching up the reins on the tines of the fork to Nelson, he cried out, "Go with what you've got."

And Nels drove to the barn. The old man stopped to roll up the rest of the windrow into rough cocks; but it was fast getting wet, and so was he, though he didn't mind that, he was so angry. He soon followed the load, a forlorn figure crossing the meadows in his shirt sleeves, with the fork on his shoulder, in a driving shower.

Trouble enough came of the quarrel in the hay-field, as Nelson had foreseen. Dick lost no time in entering a complaint against the old man, having him "hauled up," as he termed it, for assaulting him with a rake. Whereupon Podlong stepped firmly to the judge's desk, pleaded guilty, and paid his fine on the spot, with a readiness which robbed the complainant of half his revenge.

Then Dick began a suit for the recovery of wages due him, which Podlong resisted on the ground that Dick had broken his contract, and subjected him to great loss and inconvenience by striking work in the midst of a thundersquall in the hayfield.

Dick was vindictive enough to fight for his rights, in court or out, to the bitter end. But his lawyer frankly told him that the suit was likely to cost him more than he could expect to gain by it, and that by persisting in it he would punish himself more than he would hurt the old man.

"Then what shall I do?" said poor Dick despairingly.

"Settle," replied the honest attorney; "make the best terms with him you can. That's my advice to nine men out of ten who want to go to law. I'm a fool to give it, and they're fools if they don't take it. If you were rich and could afford a three or four years' fight in the courts, for the luxury of revenge, it would be different."

" I can't afford it, and he knows it," said Dick, with smouldering wrath. " If he wasn't so old a man, I'd take it out of his hide."

" Oh, that would be more foolish still!" replied the cool-headed counsel.

So Dick left the matter in his hands for settlement. But the old man was obstinate; he wouldn't pay a dollar. And at last, in a fit of disgust and despair, poor Dick, out of work and out of money, half convinced that his lawyer had been bought up by the other side, disappeared from the town.

CHAPTER III

AN UNLUCKY BASKET OF APPLES

NELS THURLOW liked Dick, and believed the old man to be in the wrong.

No doubt Podlong was secretly of the same opinion, for he was not devoid of conscience, though his stubbornness prevented him from acknowledging, even to himself sometimes, the folly of his fits of temper. They made life pretty squally at times to the boy, but he managed to dodge those little cyclones for a while ; and for weeks after his assault on Dick Stark the old man showed an extraordinary sweetness of disposition, as if by way of penance for that fault.

One day in September they were in the orchard gathering apples. Nels was at the top of a ladder in a tree filling a basket, when a huge pippin tumbled from the boughs and struck the hard orchard turf at the old man's feet.

" You careless ! " Podlong exclaimed, stooping to pick it up. " Look a' that bruise, now ! Oh, dear ! " caressing the fruit, and examining the hurt with almost as much solicitude as if it had been a child.

The boy, looking down from the top of the ladder,

couldn't but smile at the old man's anguish over a
bruised pippin.

" I couldn't help it," he said. " They fall sometimes before I can fairly get hold of 'em."

" An apple a'most as big as yer head," growled
the old man, sucking the juice from the broken
place. " Wuth as much as yer head, anyway — such
a head as yours ! "

He was stooping again to put it into a basket
when another pippin, at a touch of the boy's fingers,
slipped away before he could grasp it, struck the ladder, glanced off, and bounded to the nape of the old
man's neck, almost knocking him down.

Nels couldn't help laughing to hear him yelp, and
see him stagger under the blow. Thinking his first
care would be for the apple, he called out, " I guess
that isn't hurt much ; you kind o' broke the fall."

" Broke the fall ! " snarled the old farmer, rubbing
the back of his head with one hand, while he picked
up the apple with the other. " Well I might ; it
'most broke my neck. Laughin', be ye ? " he cried,
looking up in a great rage. " I believe ye done it
to spite me."

He appeared to be restrained from hurling the
pippin back at the boy only by a consideration of the
damage he might be doing the fruit.

" Let another come down the tree that way," he
roared, seizing hold of the ladder, " and *you'll* come
down ! "

Nels, frightened, ceased to giggle. He determined

to be extremely careful in laying hold of the next pippin. It was just beyond his reach, and, to bring it down to his hand, he pulled toward him the bough on which it hung, and on which, unluckily, he had hooked the handle of his basket.

Suddenly there was a crash. The bough broke, and down went the basket amidst a golden shower of apples tumbling about the old man's ears and shoulders, and thumping upon the ground.

The broken bough went with the basket, and the boy followed almost as quickly, eager to repair as far as possible the damage he had done.

"You villain! you critter!" shrieked old man Podlong, snatching up the bough and hurriedly stripping off the leaves and some of the twigs, "I'll larn ye!"

Nels remembered Dick Stark's misfortunes, and hastily backed off as the old man rushed upon him. He stumbled, and going down on one knee, and holding up his hands, he cried out, "Don't strike me with that! You've no right to strike me, Uncle Podlong!"

"I'll show ye whether I've a right," cried Podlong, his hat fallen with the apples, his white hair disarranged, giving him a savage aspect, and his eyes glittering. "I'm bound to give ye a thrashing!"

He had no right, indeed. He was a relative of the boy's, but not his legal guardian. Nels was an orphan who had come to work for him for seven dollars a month, and a general promise on the part

"YOU'LL BE SORRY, SIR!" — Page 233.

of the old man that he would do what was right by his sister's grandson if he would stay and do well by *him*.

He would not have been a hard master if he had not himself had the hardest of masters in the tyrannous temper whose outbursts we have witnessed. Nels had hitherto escaped his blows, and had become, in a way, a favorite with the irascible old man. But now his time had come.

He stopped backing off, and stood pale and frightened awaiting the worst.

"Uncle Podlong," he entreated, "don't! Don't, uncle!"

He had been accustomed to call the old man by that title, and he now repeated it in the hope of touching him by his last appeal. But seeing the Podlong arm raised and swung well back for a blow, he changed his tone.

"You'll be sorry, sir! I've done nothing to be whipped for, and I won't be whipped!"

"You won't, hey?" cried the furious old farmer. "Take that!" — a blow — "and that! You won't, hey? You jackanapes! How does that suit?"

CHAPTER IV

NELS FOLLOWS DICK

NELS ·cried with pain and rage, and if there had been any deadly weapon at hand he was infuriated enough to have used it for defence and vengeance. He was at first determined not to run; but the strokes rained so fast and so hard on his shoulders and sides and thighs that the resolution was quickly beaten out of him, and he turned and fled.

He was followed by the old man and the uplifted apple branch. Nels went headlong over a stone wall, behind which he regained his feet and made a stand, grasping a rock considerably too large for any boy but a young Ajax to hurl.

Podlong stopped before he reached the wall ; not, however, because he was overawed by the rock Nels lifted. One of the big pippins would have been far more dangerous in the boy's hand.

"Now come back," said the old man, "and go to work, and see if you can be a little mite less clumsy."

"I never will," Nels replied, in a white heat of passion. "I never will do another stroke of work for you as long as I live. I said I wouldn't if I had been Dick Stark, and now you've treated me worse than you did him."

And he sobbed with a sense of the wrong and ignominy that had been heaped upon him.

"Very well, do as you like," cried Podlong. "Dick didn't make much by puttin' out, and I guess you won't. The farm has got along without him, and it can get along without you."

"I'm not a slave, to be abused and knocked about by any man," Nels muttered, wishing himself a little stronger, or the rock not quite so big; there would have been such satisfaction in hurling it at the old man's head.

Thus the evil we yield to in ourselves has the power of raising a kindred demon in others, and a thoughtless blow or word may leave a lasting scar upon an innocent soul.

"I'm at work for wages, or I have been," he went on. "You owe me for over five months. But as you wouldn't pay Dick Stark" —

"I don't pay nobody that breaks his agreement with me," interrupted the old man.

"You won't give me any money?" Nels demanded.

"Nary cent!" exclaimed Podlong grimly.

"You'd better," said Nels, with a lurid fire in his eyes, as he stood bareheaded by the wall, with his disordered hair over his pale brows. "I won't stand it, and go off without my pay, as Dick did. I give you warning."

"Warning of what?" said the old man, advancing, as if to renew the flogging. "Be careful what you say."

"I know what I'm saying," returned the boy, "and I mean it."

Desperation burned in his eyes and tear-stained cheeks. There was nothing which he would not have done at that moment to avenge his wrongs, as the old man might have seen had he not been blinded by his own passion.

"Threaten me, do ye?" he retorted. "Come back to your work at once, if you know what's good for yourself."

Nels did not even return to pick up his tattered straw hat, which had been swept away by the old man's switch, but hurried along beside the wall, crossed the barnyard, and entered the house, where, reaching his garret, he began, amid sobs of rage and grief, to pack his clothes into a bundle.

CHAPTER V

MATCHES AND DRY STRAW

NELS had left his hat in the orchard, where it had fallen in his struggle with old Podlong; but he had another hat in his room. That was soon on his head; and, with his small bundle of clothes under his arm, he hurried down-stairs and through the front entry, his heart too full of passion for even a word of farewell to old Aunt Podlong.

She waylaid him, however, and asked, under her amazed spectacles, what it all meant.

"It means," said Nels, with explosive grief, "that the old man" (he was no longer *uncle*) "has whaled me," — a convulsive sob, — "and I'm going."

"O Nelson, I'm so sorry!" said the old lady soothingly. "You know he *does* give way to his temper unaccountably sometimes. I wouldn't mind it."

"Not mind it?" echoed the boy, all afire with indignation. "You don't know what it is to be licked with the limb of an apple-tree — when I wasn't to blame, either! I wouldn't stay and do another hour's work for him if it was to keep me from starving."

In vain the old lady remonstrated. Go he would;

and it was with difficulty that she could even prevail upon him to let her stuff a few doughnuts and some cheese into his bundle.

"You'll feel different after you've been away a little while," she said. "You'll come back, I guess. I'll make it all right between him and you."

"Come back? What should I ever come back for? But" — Nels faltered — "*you've* been good to me ; I haven't anything against *you*."

His voice choked again as he hurried away.

Whither he went he himself hardly knew. He avoided houses and people. Proud and sensitive, he was ashamed to let anybody see his face, the wrathful gloom of which he could not hide, and he could not have trusted himself to speak of his wrongs.

He might do as Dick Stark did, and have the old man arrested for the assault. But Podlong didn't mind walking into court and paying a little fine,— at least he pretended he didn't,— and the boy must think of some more terrible retribution. Even the wages due him, which he despaired of getting by any lawful means, seemed to him a trifle compared with the awful debt Podlong had incurred by the blows he had struck — a debt the boy vowed should be paid, at whatever cost to himself.

He sat down on the edge of a woodland, and broke spears of grass with his agitated fingers, and plotted vengeance. The sun was setting on a September landscape so fair and tranquil that it seemed a mockery to the turbulence of his heart. A laborer with

his empty dinner-pail, crossing a field a few rods below, sat down on a stone and lighted his pipe. After
smoking a few puffs he walked on, and disappeared
over the hill.

If there be such a thing as an evil genius, it must
have been that which prompted Nels to rise shortly
after and saunter down to the rock where the man
had sat. He thought he had seen something drop
from his lap as he got up, and he was not mistaken.

A fragment of a card of matches, white and clean,
lay in the grass. He looked eagerly to see if
anybody was near to observe him; then, stooping
quickly, he picked up the matches, which he carried
in his hand with an innocent air as he sauntered
back to the woods.

There, hidden in a hollow, he tried one of them on
the sole of his shoe, and found that it burned with a
lively sputter. He had three left; these he gloated
over with vindictive satisfaction, and finally put them
away carefully in his pocket. Only a short time before he had been wishing that he had taken a few
matches from Podlong's house, and wondering where
he could get some.

A gray squirrel skipped along the ground, so near
that he could have knocked it over if he had thrown
his bundle at it. But he hardly saw it; his mind
was filled with a vision of fire and smoke, — a blazing farm-yard, barn and stacks and sheds going up
in roaring flames in a midnight sky, and old man

Podlong rushing out with shrieks of rage at sight of his burning property.

How Nels passed the time until eleven o'clock that night I hardly know. At that gloomy hour a slight dark figure, visible only to the eyes of the calm stars, crept stealthily under the shadow of a huge straw-stack standing within two rods of Podlong's great barn.

It was the figure of a boy. The boy was Nels Thurlow.

Having reached a sheltered spot under the brow of the stack, he concealed himself and listened. All was still in the house. Uncle and Aunt Podlong and their hired girl were no doubt sleeping soundly.

All had been quiet, too, in the house of Gideon Shaw, their nearest neighbor, when Nels passed it a few minutes before. Only the rhythmical chorus of the tree crickets broke the stillness of the autumn night.

After waiting and listening a while, he pulled out armfuls of straw from the stack, until he had a pile breast-high beside him. This, after another long pause, he carried and heaped against the corner of the barn. Some got scattered by the way, and he now scattered more over the same ground, until there was a continuous trail of straw between the barn and the stack.

Everything, from the finding of the matches, seemed to favor the boy's scheme of vengeance.

He remembered hearing Podlong say, only two

days before, that the insurance on his buildings had run out, and that he must get it renewed the first time he went to the village. He had not gone to the village yet, unless he went that afternoon. And the barn was filled with hay to the tops of the mows, and with grain to the edge of the great bins,— wheat and oats and rye, — while the floor was heaped with still unhusked corn.

CHAPTER VI

THE MAN WITH A LADDER

THERE were also adjoining sheds with lofts crammed with fodder; wagons and sleighs in the wagon house, and ploughs and harrows and machines and tools wherever they could be best stowed away.

Under the open sheds and in the yard were sleeping cattle. Nels had no grudge against them; he went softly and let down the bars leading into a lane, so that they could escape at the first alarm. There was a stable nearer the house, but that he would spare for the sake of the horses it sheltered. The house, too, should be exempt, because of the old lady's last kind words to him, although she had not always been so kind.

When all was ready he sat down again under the stack to fortify his resolution with recollections of the wrong he had endured, and to enjoy in anticipation the old man's impotent fury at the sight of his blazing property. He did not much care what might happen to himself. He believed he could escape; but, even at the risk of being caught and punished, he was determined to have his revenge.

While he was waiting, and hardening his heart as

often as it whispered to him that what he was doing
was desperately dangerous and wicked, a noise in the
direction of the orchard drew his attention. Was
the old man out there picking his precious pippins
at that time of night?

He had certainly heard a bough clash, and a thump
on the ground, as of one of the great apples in its
fall. Silence followed for a few minutes; only the
crickets kept up their pulsing song, and now and
then a full-fed cow in the yard heaved a far-heard
sigh of content. Then came an unmistakable noise
at the orchard wall.

Nels lay perfectly still, thrilling with a strange
fear, and all his senses strained by intense excitement.
Presently a man got over the wall and stood in the
starlit gloom not more than five or six rods away —
so far, indeed, that Nels would not have seen him but
for the sound that attracted and quickened his sight
in the obscurity.

After another pause the man drew over the fence
something which, by his movements and the slight
rubbing sound it made, Nells guessed to be a ladder
— probably the same from which he had picked the
fatal pippins that afternoon.

He crept out of his hiding-place, and, following at
a safe distance, saw the man approach the house,
raise the ladder, and place it noiselessly against one
of the upper windows. There the robber — for such
he undoubtedly was — waited a long time, as it
seemed to Nels, and finally, mounting softly, tried

the sash. It seemed to offer no difficulties, and soon his head and shoulders, which showed black against the white-painted side of the house, disappeared in the room.

All this had served to divert the boy's mind from his own private scheme of vengeance. And now, crouched behind a quince-bush, he had leisure for other reflections. What satisfaction would it be to him that the old man should suffer from a robbery at the hands of one whom he had probably never wronged?

Far from being a bad boy at heart, Nelson Thurlow had an unusually strong sense of justice. It was that which had been so deeply outraged by Podlong's ill-treatment of him, and driven him wild with the desire of vengeance. But the same feeling which in its lower manifestations may prompt revenge, in its nobler aspect is conscience. And how could Nelson's conscience let him lurk there while old man Podlong was being robbed?

When he used to sleep in the next room to the one the burglar was entering (that had been Dick Stark's), how eager he would have been to defend the house against any such depredation! The old feeling came back upon him, and he half forgot his own injuries in a sudden impulse to baffle the burglar.

But what should he do? Try to alarm the family, and by an outcry give him warning and a chance to escape? Better run back to Gideon Shaw's house, get assistance, and help to capture the rogue. Although he had himself been wrought up to the commission of a dreadful deed, Nels had no sympathy with robbers, or with rogues of any sort.

Gideon Shaw lived hardly forty rods away, and in less than three minutes Nels was knocking at his door.

CHAPTER VII

PODLONG'S CONSCIENCE

PODLONG had not slept well for an hour or two after going to bed. Stoutly as he was accustomed to bear himself after his fits of passion, he often felt more remorse for them than he was willing anybody should suspect, and he was particularly disturbed by the recollection of his mad abuse of Nelson. He had sharply cut short his wife's remonstrance; but he could not quiet his own thoughts so easily.

"I hadn't ought to have flogged him," he said to himself, as he turned on his pillow, trying in vain to sleep.

"Why *can't* I learn to keep a curb on my pesky temper? He's re'ly the best-intentioned boy I ever had on the farm, and I might have had a little patience, 'stead o' wallopin' on him."

He groaned and turned again, wondering if he was keeping Mrs. Podlong awake.

"Now I've lost him, I s'pose! for 'tain't likely a boy o' his sperit'll come back. And he's lost a good place; for I'd 'ave done well by him if he'd stayed. He's jest the boy I want. What possessed me to be so hash with him, I can't understand!"

The remorseful Podlong tried to comfort himself with the reflection that he would try to find Nelson the next day and bring him back ; inwardly vowing, for I suppose the thousandth time in his life, that he would never let his temper get away with him again. In the midst of these thoughts he fell asleep, to be awakened not long after by a violent knock at the door.

"Who's there ? " he shouted, starting up in bed. And at the same moment he was aware of a man leaping up from the floor and darting out of the room.

" Robbers ! — there's robbers in your house ! " the knocker stopped knocking to shout.

The old man, calling to his wife not to be frightened, sprang in his night-clothes to a tall bureau, behind which stood an old musket. It wasn't loaded ; and even if it had been, it would have proved a dangerous weapon to the man trying to fire it. But the but-end might be useful to strike with ; and thus armed, Podlong rushed out in pursuit of the intruder.

After getting in at the chamber window, the robber had cautiously made his way down-stairs, and entered the old folks' sleeping-room, which was on the lower floor. The old man commonly carried a thick roll of bank-bills in his pocket-book ; and it was this the fellow was after. He had barely got his hand upon it when the alarm came at the front door, and the farmer sprang out of bed.

At the back door Nels was standing guard, with an

eye turned up at the window where he had seen the
man's legs, following his head and shoulders, disappear
in the house. Precisely at the moment when the
alarm was raised in front he pulled down the ladder,
and made a highly strategic use of it at the back door.
He turned it up on its edge against the steps, which
he had hardly done when the house-breaker, having
unbolted the door on the inside, opened it, dashed
out, and plunged headlong over the ladder, which
tripped his feet in a most unexpected fashion.

The old man rushed out after him, full of fight,
with his clubbed musket ready to do execution upon
a whole band of robbers.

As the man stumbled over the ladder, Nels flung
himself on his back to prevent him from rising, and
screamed for help. The old man saw the two struggling figures, and, not knowing which head to hit,
threw away his musket. At the same time Gideon
Shaw came hurrying around the house, with an iron
rake in his hands and a whip-lash in his pocket.

Between the three the burglar was captured and
bound; and by the time this feat was accomplished
Aunt Podlong came to the door with a lighted lamp.

"Is this you, Nelson?" said the old man in an agitated voice, as the gleam fell upon the boy's face.

Out of breath with his recent struggle, Nels did
not speak. But the helpful neighbor had a voice, and
used it.

"He saw the robber getting into a window, and
came to my house and gave the alarm. He has had

the hardest part of the tussle ; but my whip-lash has come handy."

"Nelson," said the old man, trembling in his night-clothes, "you've done me a turn I'd no right to expect. I believe the rascal has my pocket-book ; leastwise, he had pulled my trousers off 'm the foot-board, where I always hang 'em when I go to bed. Must be some-body who knows the house. Turn round here, you scamp, and le's look at your face! Dick Stark!"

"Yes, sir ; Dick Stark," said the man, boldly con-fronting him. "You think I came to rob you. No, sir ; I came to help myself to the money you owe me, since I couldn't come by it any other way. And I might have got off with some of it, at least, if it hadn't been for Nels."

"Dick!" exclaimed the old man, "I never believed you would do such a thing!"

"I wouldn't, if your beating and cheating me hadn't driven me to it," replied Dick.

"That's no excuse," said Podlong. "Look at Nels, here. I used him, this very day, wuss'n ever I did you. But 'stead o' comin' back to rob me, he comes to save me from robbers."

"Uncle," spoke up Nels, in a choking voice, "I didn't come back to do you a good turn. And I'll tell you the truth. If I had known it was Dick after his pay I wouldn't have interfered."

"You think he was doing right?"

The old man was a strange-looking object, standing in the lamplight, with his white hair and excited features, and a many-colored bed-quilt, which his wife brought him, wrapped about his shivering limbs.

"No, not right," said Nels. "But you know, uncle, how you had treated him."

He spoke earnestly, and not without fear of what his words might provoke. But Podlong was not angry.

They were in the kitchen by this time; and Aunt Podlong, dreading the effect of the cold air on the old man's naked shanks, closed the door.

"Untie his hands, Gideon," said Podlong in a shaking voice. "Now give me my pocket-book, Dick. If there's money enough in it, and I guess there is,— for I've been savin' some to pay my insurance,— you shall have your dues this very night. I hain't done right myself; I know it, and I don't mind sayin' it here in the presence of you all. Count out his money, Gideon — I can't — with somethin', whatever he thinks is right, for the trouble and expense I've put him to."

It was pitiful to see him so humiliated and broken; and when he turned and said, "Now, Nelson, boy, what can I do for you?" the lad's heart went out to him with a throb of sympathy and pity.

"Nothing, uncle; I am all right," he said in a suffocated voice, and with tear-blinded eyes.

"Well, then, go to bed. You'd better turn in too, Dick. And, Gideon, you've had to suffer sometimes from my temper, as well as the rest of 'em; but I vow you never shall again!"

So Nels returned to the little room which he had not expected ever to see again. In his gratitude, as he crept into his bed, and felt that he was once more at home, he could not but wonder if he was the same boy who an hour ago had skulked behind the stack in pursuit of a horrible revenge. What satisfaction could there have been in that? How hideous the very thought of it, compared with the bliss of forgiving and being forgiven!

He slept little that night, so anxious was he to get out at daybreak and clear up the litter around the stack before the old man, or even Dick Stark, should see it.

This he did, and had got the straw mostly back in a heap under the brow of the stack when the old man appeared.

"So! this is the bed you made for yourself last night," was Podlong's innocent comment. "I'm glad enough Dick come along to disturb you."

"So am I," said the contrite boy.

IN A CALIFORNIA CAÑON

CHAPTER I

HOW THE STORY CAME TO BE TOLD

MINISTERS are not a class of men who are generally supposed to have met with any very startling
adventures. Yet one of this peaceful calling, whose
acquaintance I made a few years ago on a journey to
Northern Michigan, had had in his boyhood an encounter which, in vivid frightfulness, as he related
it, I think is rarely surpassed.

He was a slight, mild, unassuming man, with one
arm noticeably shorter than the other. Some allu-
sion to this peculiarity from one of our party —
we were on the after-deck of a Lake Superior steamboat plying between ports on the south shore and
Duluth — called out from him the story, which I
shall give substantially as he told it.

CHAPTER II

WITH PONY AND GUN

My uncle's sheep ranch (said our fellow traveller) was situated in the valley of a small stream which flows out from the spurs of the Sierra Nevada, and falls into one of the northern tributaries of the Sacramento. There I visited him, in company with my mother, in the summer of my sixteenth year.

I had a spinal affection, which made me a puny boy; and it was in the hope that a change of climate might benefit my health, that a pressing invitation from our California relatives was accepted, and we went to spend a year on the Pacific slope.

Under the influence of the new, wild life of the ranch my health began to improve immediately; and my friends declared that they could actually see me grow!

There was room enough for that, for at that time I was so small I was almost ashamed to tell people my age. Still, it must have been my fresher complexion and brighter spirits, rather than a slight increase in stature, that gained from my friends, in a few weeks, that delightful compliment. I believe there is nothing else so gratifying to a stunted boy as to be told that he is growing.

In urging our visit, my uncle had promised me a pony and a gun. These excited my most ardent expectations; though I can't say that they proved quite such powerful inducements to the mind of my anxious mother. She dreaded to have her darling touch a gun; she shuddered at the mere thought of me mounted on the back of a horse!

But when she came to see me shoot at a mark, and meet with no worse mishap than to miss it, which I did, of course, and actually ride the pretty little pony my uncle had provided for me, she conquered her timidity, and became willing at last to entrust me out of her sight. I galloped over the range, and along the sparsely wooded banks of the stream, hunting grouse, rabbits, and other small game; and although I brought home few trophies of the chase, I always returned in such a glow from healthy exercise, that my mother became quite reconciled to the sport.

Still she cautioned me not to ride "too far away;" an injunction which I fully intended to heed. But as my powers of endurance increased, my ideas of distance enlarged; until one day I met with the adventure I am going to relate.

I didn't exactly aspire to encounter a grizzly; but it was my ambition to shoot a deer, a mountain sheep, or at least a coyote. To ride home some day and announce to my mother and uncle and charming Cousin Ruth that I had slain a wolf, even if it were only one of that small cowardly western species, would have made me feel myself about as big as any boy.

A sheep would now and then get astray, in spite of the shepherds ; when it was pretty sure to be killed within a few hours by some marauding beast or beasts from the mountains. To repay my uncle's kindness by helping to rid the range of these pests, was another motive for extending my excursions.

One morning I actually startled some wild creature from its prey, in a clump of cotton-woods, on the banks of the stream.

I hardly had a glimpse of it as it darted behind a ledge and disappeared. It must have been much larger than a coyote ; and I concluded that it was a real wolf, never having seen one in my life.

The skittishness of my pony prevented me from dashing on and getting a better view of the fugitive. I was excited, and maybe a little scared. I paused to withdraw the small shot from one barrel of my fowling-piece, and ram down an ounce ball instead. The other barrel already had a charge of buck. I remember how my hands shook as I performed that simple operation.

Then I urged my pony into the clump of trees out of which the beast had leaped, and saw one of my uncle's fine merinos partially devoured. The shyness of the horse I supposed to be occasioned by the smell of blood. There may have been something in that ; but he was also repelled from the spot by a wilder instinct, which had been transmitted to him by his Mexican progenitors, and of which I had a more awkward experience before long.

I did not get near enough to examine the animal's tracks about the carcass, or I might not have started off quite so eagerly as I did in pursuit of such game.

The hills toward which it had fled rose in broken and scantily wooded masses about a mile beyond. Still farther, above the slopes and crags of those spurs, rose other slopes and crags, with vaporous chasms and verdurous crests, peak beyond peak, to the snowy scalps of the Sierras; which in the distance, to my boyish eyes, resembled delicately tinted mountains of ice-cream.

I galloped off, keeping within sight of the stream, and following it up into the gorge through which it issued from the foothills. I was soon in the cool shadows of the cliffs, with the torrent plunging over its rocky bed beside me, twenty feet below.

Cotton-woods, willows, birches, and other forest trees grew wherever they could get a foothold among the rocks ; and the loveliest wild-flowers imaginable smiled up at me from the natural pathway at the base of the cliffs along which I rode.

The gorge was full of bowlders and broken blocks, among which I looked cautiously for game as I proceeded. A few Rocky Mountain jays screamed in the tree-tops. A red-shafted woodpecker — the same birds as your eastern golden-shafted species, except that it has red markings where the other has yellow — flitted before me ; and a jack-rabbit invited my shot from the opposite bank of the stream. But I reserved my lead for larger game.

The gorge, which was perhaps a hundred yards wide at the entrance, broadened farther on into a glen of wonderful wildness and beauty, and then narrowed again to a cañon cut through the very heart of the hills. I had been in the glen before with my uncle ; but now for the first time I pushed farther on up into the cañon.

I was glancing down at the tumbling torrent, or up at the broken pine-crowned slopes, — all the time keeping a sharp lookout for game, — and my sure-footed pony was picking his way at will over the stones and among the blocks and bowlders that strewed the bank of the stream, when suddenly he pricked up his ears, gave a frightened snuff, and stopped.

I let go the reins, and poised my gun, trembling at the sudden prospect of game, the scent of which had no doubt alarmed Roland.

Still I could see nothing ; and his mysterious conduct filled me with a vague terror. He was snorting and backing; and I was about resuming the reins, to head him away from the danger, down the gorge, when all at once, stealthy, silent, crouching, a wild animal appeared on a ledge of the cliff, less than twenty feet before me.

CHAPTER III

IN THE LAIR OF THE LIONESS

I KNEW the creature at a glance. It was an American lion, or rather lioness, and one of the very largest size. A heap of rocks had hidden her from view until she was in the very act of preparing for a spring.

I can think of no word to express what I felt at that terrible moment. It was no ordinary fear; it was a sort of paralysis, which so froze and benumbed me that I could neither take aim with my gun nor effect a retreat.

But in that moment the scene was photographed on my memory; and now, shutting my eyes, I can see again the monster's softly gliding approach, the quick, nervous movement of her forward-reaching paw on the rocks, her great catlike eyes, her writhing tail, even the beautiful white of her breast !

It could have been but a moment, when I recovered myself sufficiently to raise my gun. But before I could fire, Roland, who had already backed half around, suddenly gave a wild snort and a sideways leap, and darted from under me. I remember making an ineffectual clutch at mane and saddle ; then all is a blank to me, for I know not how many minutes.

In falling I must have struck my head upon a stone, and become insensible for that blessed interval. On opening my eyes again, the first thing I consciously saw was an inverted tree moving past me, against the background of a cliff, where there were more moving, inverted trees.

I was wondering vaguely at this, when I perceived that it was my own body that was in motion. I was being dragged along the edge of a bank, over which my head was helplessly hanging.

Strange as it may seem, I no longer felt the deadly fright which had so appalled me at first. I knew that I was in the clutch of the most ferocious of our wild beasts ; one that had been known to kill even the enormous grizzly bear in open fight. But I remained passive, powerless, almost reconciled to my fate.

I expected nothing less than that I should be dragged to some spot that suited the creature's ideas of convenience and safety, and there eaten at her leisure. And when once she snarlingly laid me down, and lifted her head to look around, I said to myself quietly, " My time has come ! "

She had been carrying me by the folds of my hunting-jacket, which was of strong velveteen, fitting loosely. I couldn't feel that I was seriously injured as yet ; and that discovery revived in me a desire to live.

I thought of my mother and friends with an indescribable rush of emotions, — fear and longing and despair ; and made a movement, to learn if I still had the use of my limbs.

That movement was instantly answered by so deep and savage a growl from the lioness, that I did not venture to make another. She clapped a paw upon my shoulder, while her fangs met again in the folds of my jacket ; crouching over me in an attitude which convinced me that I was immediately to be torn in pieces. The side of her muzzle and one great flaming eye were close to my face ; her whiskers tickled my cheek.

Instead of tearing me, however, she presently began to drag me again, lifting my head and shoulders clear from the ground. My legs trailed ; my heels knocked on the stones. I looked up into the whitish under fur of her powerful sideways-turned neck, and felt at every step the working of her shoulder-bone against my side.

She not only carried me in this manner with seeming ease, but, coming to the face of a rock several feet high, she leaped up with me, as a cat might leap to a window-sill with a kitten in her mouth.

I remember distinctly nothing more, until something darkened over me ; it was a heavily projecting ledge from the brow of a cavern, in the shadow of which she laid me down again, growling, and giving my shoulder a couple of sharp taps with her paw.

These were intended, I thought, to see if I was

still alive. But I made no motion, although I felt her claws pierce through to my flesh. I lay partly on my left side, with my feet toward the mouth of the cave ; and I could look out into the boughs of a spruce-tree that grew on the slope. I shall never forget how strange a shaft of sunshine appeared, slanting through those boughs !

Unhappily, I could also see objects within the cave, not agreeable to contemplate. Right before my eyes lay a couple of well-gnawed bones on the littered floor.

Mingled with the beast's growling I heard other sounds which, together with the uncanny sight of the bones, filled me with fresh terror. Mysterious, indescribable, they proceeded from the depths of the cave, — harsh, hungry, mewing, and whining cries, as if the hollow behind me had been packed full of savage creatures, tumbling over and smothering one another.

These noises grew less muffled, and seemed to approach nearer ; then three furry creatures, about the size of common cats, but much clumsier, came crawling over and about me, sniffing at my clothes and uttering again their harsh, whining mews.

I was in the lair of the lioness, whither I had been dragged to furnish sport for her young and practice for their infant teeth.

Fortunately my clothing was not much to their taste. They turned to her with a ravenous importunity, to which she yielded; and there, in my sight, stretching herself out on the floor of the cave, she gave them suck.

The mind is so constituted that we soon grow accustomed to things that seem at first too painful or too terrible to be endured. I took in fully the dreadful peril of my position; but I had regained possession of my faculties, and was capable of observing all that took place.

As the lioness lay before me on the ground, I could see what a lithe, alert, superb, tremendous animal she was. Her head, lifted upright over one foreshoulder, was opposite my knees; her hind feet stretched out beyond my face. Between her and me were her kittens, — or whelps as we should call them if the beast were really a lion. But though dignified by that name in California, where it grows to a truly formidable size, — a name suggested also by the leonine color of the upper portions of its body, — the animal is really the cougar, or puma, or panther of other parts of America.

Notwithstanding my fearfully anxious state of mind, I noticed that the young ones were differently marked from the mother. They too had white, or grayish white, below; but, above, their fur was of a lighter tint than hers, which was reddish brown; and they had rows of pretty, soft black streaks and spots on their sides.

She seemed proud and fond of them, and purred as they nestled in her breast. Such a purr! Its low, slow thunder filled the cave. Now and then she put down her head and rubbed her face and the upper side of her neck against their backs.

They left her breast now and then to crawl over her, or tussle with each other, returning to it after each tumble, and tugging away again at her teats until their hunger was satisfied.

Then commenced a frolic so catlike that I was at one time almost led to hope that I might gain some advantage from their good-nature.

Yet I knew well that I owed my respite not to that, but to the simple fact that the mother had but lately gorged her appetite for flesh and blood, and that her young ones' first preference was for milk. She was sure to be hungry again before long ; and she would then, no doubt, give them a lesson in dis- posing of their prey. Meanwhile, I was a morsel that would keep.

She probably thought me disabled, as I certainly should have been but for my clothing, which had served as a foil to her fiercely meeting fangs. Yet, even while occupied with her young, I felt that she never for a moment lost sight of me with those wild, vigilant eyes.

I lay as she had left me, not daring to stir, but beginning at length to question whether there might not yet be for me some chance of escape.

CHAPTER IV

THE RESCUE

THE sole weapon I had about me was a common pocket-knife; but even though I could have managed to get at that and open it without exciting her attention, I felt that it would be a mere toy in a combat with such a foe. And any attempt to get away from the cave, either by agility or stealth, would only have precipitated my fate.

I was four miles from the ranch; it would be hours yet before my absence would cause much anxiety, and even then who would think of looking for me in the lair of a lioness?

In their gambols the kittens sometimes brushed my face with their tails; and once the mad impulse seized me to catch one and pitch it over the ledge at the mouth of the cave, in the hope that the mother would follow it. Then I might fling the other two still farther down into the cañon, and, while she was looking them up, make my escape.

It was a desperate thought; but my situation was desperate, and sudden death seemed better than the prolonged agony of suspense, which, after all, death must end.

If I had been in a position to take sudden hold of one of the young ones ; if there had been room, as the saying is, to " swing a cat," and I had had time to do it before the mother could hinder me, I think I should have made the attempt.

I saw how impossible it was.   Then, again, I hoped she would soon tire of her play, and, stupefied perhaps by her recent banquet, lie down to digest it, and go to sleep ; thus affording me one chance in a thousand to creep out without awaking her.

After a while she seemed inclined to rest.   She dropped her muzzle on her paws, and only started up now and then to cuff her young ones when they continued to tumble over her.

Then suddenly one of them turned its attention to me.   The others followed its example.   They nipped at my clothing, and I could feel their sharp teeth pricking into my flesh.

It was a moment of intense, torturing expectation. The lioness looked on with sleepy, half-shut eyes.   I fancied I could see in her feline features an expression of tranquil enjoyment and approval, as her kits began to tear their prey.

They had torn not much else but my clothing, when one of them came pouncing at my face.   I couldn't stand that.   Besides, I felt sure that, once they had fairly tasted blood, they would soon make an end of me if I didn't resist ; or she would despatch me if I did.

I was afraid to use anything like violence ; and the

playfulness of the little panther encouraged me to think that gentle resistance might. avail. I put my arm about it, to hold it back from my face, and instinctively, as if the creature had. been a domestic cat, stroked its head with my hand. I remember feeling a fearful, prayerful, pleading, hopeless sort of hope, that it might accept my caress, and that I might even gain the mother's good-will by my attentions to her young!

I might better have undertaken to tame the maddest torrent of the Sierras, and have trusted myself to its mercies!

The little spitfire gave a snarl as it sprang back from me; and at the instant, sudden, noiseless, swift, the lioness leaped up. She was on me at a bound, uttering one deep growl, as her open jaws, with their backward-drawn lips and glittering teeth, closed upon my shoulder and clung.

It is a fearful thing to hear one's own flesh and bone crush and crunch; but that is what I heard with horrible distinctness at that moment. I don't remember so much the physical pain I must have suffered; but I felt a sort of despairing pity of myself as I lay powerless in that cruel clutch.

What happened for the next quarter of an hour I know only by hearsay; for when my friends found me I was in a swoon.

My uncle was riding over the range with a couple of visitors, when my pony came galloping down toward them from the hills. The direction of his flight indicating the gorge, they rode up into it, and were still further guided in their search for me by the discovery of my gun, some drops of blood, and finally by the marks made by my body trailed along the ground.

Their shouts filled the cañon as they advanced; and the lioness must have taken alarm while in the very act of rending me. In her anxiety to defend her lair and her young, she issued forth, and showed herself on a projection of the cliff, where a couple of well-aimed shots brought her tumbling into the gorge.

What my mother suffered when I was taken home to her in a mangled, and, as she believed, dying condition, I wouldn't undertake to tell, if I could. My shoulder was so broken that it never quite came into place again; and, as you have noticed, I carry my left arm differently from the other to this day.

With surgical aid and the kindest nursing, however, I recovered from my hurts; and, strange to say, from my spinal troubles at the same time.

The young panthers were ruthlessly killed in the excitement of my rescue; although I think my uncle always regretted — as I did — that my critical condition allowed no time for the capture of one or two of them alive.

The mother, as I have already said, was one of the largest of her kind, measuring four feet ten and a half inches from her nose to her tail, which measured

I forget how much more. My uncle had her hide made into a rug for my mother ; but she never could endure the sight of it, — and no wonder ! It is now in the possession of my Cousin Ruth, who is the wife of a merchant of San Francisco.

THE END

THE TIDE-MILL STORIES

Six Volumes. Handsomely Illustrated. Per Vol., $1.25.

THE TINKHAM BROTHERS' TIDE-MILL
PHIL AND HIS FRIENDS
THE SATIN-WOOD BOX
THE LITTLE MASTER
HIS ONE FAULT
PETER BUDSTONE

"The more stories Mr. Trowbridge can write, the better for the boys of this generation. Flooded as our country is with literature of a dime-novel order, we have need of just such safe and interesting books as 'The Little Master,' 'Phil and His Friends,' 'Bound in Honor,' etc., to put into the hands of our growing boys."--*Living Church.*

"Mr. Trowbridge's humor, his fidelity to nature and story-telling power, lose nothing with years, and he stands at the head of those who are furnishing a literature for the young, clean and sweet in tone, and always of interest and value."--*The Continent.*

LEE AND SHEPARD Publishers Boston

SILVER MEDAL STORIES

Six Volumes. Handsomely Illustrated. Per Vol., $1.25.

THE SILVER MEDAL

HIS OWN MASTER

BOUND IN HONOR

THE POCKET-RIFLE

THE JOLLY ROVER

YOUNG JOE AND OTHER BOYS

"If every boy could read these stories, or have them read to him, there would be fewer rogues in the world. Straightforward, honest stories, without cant, without moralizing, full of genuine fun and hard common sense, they are just the tales that are needed to make a young fellow fall in love with simple integrity and fair dealing. They are noble contributions to juvenile literature."— *Woman's Journal.*

"Mr. Trowbridge has a good perception of character, which he draws with skill; he has abundance of invention, which he never abuses; and he has, what so many American writers have not, an easy, graceful style, which can be humorous, or pathetic, or poetic."—*R. H. Stoddard in N. Y. Mail.*

LEE AND SHEPARD Publishers Boston

THE FORTUNES OF TOBY TRAFFORD.

Cloth.   Illustrated. $1.25.

A new story by J. T. Trowbridge, is, like all Mr. Trowbridge's fiction, the good wine that needs no bush. The plot is full of interest, and is still so natural that it all might happen in a thousand places. Its scenes and its people are everywhere ; only few writers have Trowbridge's eyes to see them. The hero is not an impossibly good boy, but he has manly instincts ; and he is kept from follies and mistakes by the counsels of an excellent mother, and of his wise and noble-hearted schoolmaster. Boys will follow his career and his good and bad fortune with genuine interest. — *Boston Budget.*

FATHER BRIGHTHOPES

OR

AN OLD CLERGYMAN'S VACATION.

NEW AND REVISED EDITION, WITH AUTOBIOGRAPHICAL PREFACE.

Cloth.   Illustrated. $1.25.

To the many new friends which this book will doubtless gain it may be well to say that Father Brighthopes of the story gains that cheery name by his readiness to always see the bright and not the dark side of any difficulty great or small. The few weeks which he spent with his friends the Roydens wrought a change in their daily life as marked as it was pleasant. The writings of Trowbridge are too well known to require comment, since almost everyone is familiar with his straightforward, simple style, underlying which there is not a little humor as well as pathos. The present edition of "Father Brighthopes" is neatly bound and contains several fair illustrations among the pages which embody so many useful lessons, more especially for young people, who have yet time to profit by its teachings. — *Chicago Times.*

THE BLUE AND THE GRAY

SERIES

Illustrated. With Emblematic Dies. Each volume bound in Blue and Gray. Per volume, $1.50.

TAKEN BY THE ENEMY.
WITHIN THE ENEMY'S LINES.
ON THE BLOCKADE.
STAND BY THE UNION.
FIGHTING FOR THE RIGHT.
THE VICTORIOUS UNION.

The opening of a new series of books from the pen of Oliver Optic is bound to arouse the highest anticipation in the minds of boy and girl readers. There never has been a more interesting writer in the field of juvenile literature than Mr. W. T. Adams, who, under his well-known pseudonym, is known and admired by every boy and girl in the country, and by thousands who have long since passed the boundaries of youth, yet who remember with pleasure the genial, interesting pen that did so much to interest, instruct and entertain their younger years. The present volume opens " The Blue and the Gray Series," a title that is sufficiently indicative of the nature and spirit of the series, of which the first volume is now presented, while the name of Oliver Optic is sufficient warrant of the absorbing style of narrative. " Taken by the Enemy," the first book of the series, is as bright and entertaining as any work that Mr. Adams has yet put forth, and will be as eagerly perused as any that has borne his name. It would not be fair to the prospective reader to deprive him of the zest which comes from the unexpected, by entering into a synopsis of the story. A word, however, should be said in regard to the beauty and appropriateness of the binding, which makes it a most attractive volume.—*Boston Budget.*

" Taken by the Enemy " has just come from the press, an announcement that cannot but appeal to every healthy boy from ten to fifteen years of age in the country. "No writer of the present day," says the Boston *Commonwealth,* "whose aim has been to hit the boyish heart, has been as successful as Oliver Optic. There is a period in the life of every youth, just about the time that he is collecting postage-stamps, and before his legs are long enough for a bicycle, when he has the Oliver Optic fever. He catches it by reading a few stray pages somewhere, and then there is nothing for it but to let the matter take its course Relief comes only when the last page of the last book is read; and then there are relapses whenever a new book appears until one is safely on through the teens." — *Literary News.*

www.ingramcontent.com/pod-product-compliance
Lightning Source LLC
Chambersburg PA
CBHW031409270326
41929CB00010BA/1381